AN ANTHOLOGY OF
TWENTIETH-CENTURY
NEW ZEALAND POETRY

AN ANTHOLOGY OF
TWENTIETH-CENTURY NEW ZEALAND POETRY

Selected by
VINCENT O'SULLIVAN

LONDON
OXFORD UNIVERSITY PRESS
NEW YORK   WELLINGTON
1970

Oxford University Press, Ely House, London W.1

GLASGOW NEW YORK TORONTO MELBOURNE WELLINGTON
CAPE TOWN SALISBURY IBADAN NAIROBI DAR ES SALAAM LUSAKA ADDIS ABABA
BOMBAY CALCUTTA MADRAS KARACHI LAHORE DACCA
KUALA LUMPUR SINGAPORE HONG KONG TOKYO

Hardbound edition SBN 19 211290 2
Paperbound edition SBN 19 281092 8

*First published by Oxford University Press, London,
simultaneously in hard covers and as an
Oxford University Press paperback, 1970*

*Printed in Great Britain by
Richard Clay (The Chaucer Press), Ltd.,
Bungay, Suffolk*

821. 90082

AN 6

CONTENTS

v

38936

vii

ix

x

xiv

ACKNOWLEDGEMENTS

For permission to reproduce copyright passages grateful acknowledgement is made to the publishers and copyright holders of the following:

Arthur Adams, *Maoriland: and other Verses* (The Bulletin Newspaper Co., Sydney, 1899).

Fleur Adcock, *The Eye of the Hurricane* (A. H. & A. W. Reed, 1964).

K. O. Arvidson, *Landfall* (vols. 68, 71, 73, 88, 1963, 1964, 1965, and 1968, and the Author).

B. E. Baughan, *Reuben and Other Poems* (Constable, 1903); *Shingle-short and Other Verses* (Whitcombe & Tombs, 1908).

James K. Baxter, *The Lion Skin* (University of Otago, 1967).

Mary Ursula Bethell, *Collected Poems* (Caxton Press, 1950).

Peter Bland, *My Side of the Story, Poems 1960–64* (Mate Books, 1964); *London Magazine* (vol. 6, February 1967, and the Author).

Charles Brasch, *Disputed Ground, Poems 1939–45* (Caxton Press, 1948); *The Estate and Other Poems* (Caxton Press, 1957); *Ambulando* (Caxton Press, 1964); *Not Far Off* (Caxton Press, 1969).

Alistair Campbell, *Blue Rain* (Wai-te-ata Press, 1967); *The New Zealand Listener* (vol. 61, 1969, and the Author).

Gordon Challis, *Building* (Caxton Press, 1963).

Allen Curnow, *Island and Time* (Caxton Press, 1941).

Ruth Dallas, *Country Road and Other Poems, 1947–52* (Caxton Press, 1953); *The Turning Wheel* (Caxton Press, 1961); *Day Book* (Caxton Press, 1966); *Shadow Show* (Caxton Press, 1968).

Basil Dowling, *Signs and Wonders* (Caxton Press, 1944); *Canterbury and Other Poems* (Caxton Press, 1949); *Landfall* (vol. 30, 1954).

Charles Doyle, *A Splinter of Glass* (Pegasus Press, 1967); *Distances*

xv

(Paul's Book Arcade, 1963); *Messages for Herod* (Collins, 1965).

Eileen Duggan, *Poems* (Allen & Unwin, 1937); *More Poems* (Allen & Unwin, 1951, and the Author).

A. R. D. Fairburn, *Collected Poems* (Pegasus Press, 1966).

Janet Frame, *The Pocket Mirror* (Pegasus Press, 1967).

Denis Glover, *The Wind and the Sand* (Caxton Press, 1945); *Sings Harry and Other Poems* (Caxton Press, 1951); *Arawata Bill: A Sequence of Poems* (Pegasus Press, 1953).

Paul Henderson, *Unwilling Pilgrim* (Caxton Press, 1955); *The Halting Place* (Caxton Press, 1961).

J. R. Hervey, *New Poems* (Caxton Press, 1940); *Man on a Raft, More Poems* (Caxton Press, 1949); *Landfall* (vol. 35, 1955).

Robin Hyde, *Houses by the Sea and the Later Poems of Robin Hyde* (Caxton Press, 1952).

Kevin Ireland, *Face to Face* (Pegasus Press, 1963); *Educating the Body* (Caxton Press, 1967).

Michael Jackson, *Landfall* (vols. 75, 83, 1965 and 1967, and the Author).

Louis Johnson, *Poems Unpleasant* (with others, Pegasus Press, 1952); *New Worlds for Old* (Capricorn Press, 1957); *Bread and a Pension* (Pegasus Press, 1964).

M. K. Joseph, *New Zealand Poetry Year Book* (Pegasus Press, 1954); *The Living Countries* (Paul's Book Arcade, 1959); *Imaginary Islands* (1950, by permission of the Author).

Owen Leeming, *Recent Poetry in New Zealand* (Collins, 1965).

Katherine Mansfield, *Poems* (Constable, 1923); *To Stanislaw Wyspianski* (Bodley Head, 1938, the Society of Authors, and Alfred A. Knopf Inc.).

R. A. K. Mason, *Collected Poems* (Pegasus Press, 1962).

W. H. Oliver, *Fire Without Phoenix, Poems 1946–54* (Caxton Press, 1957).

Vincent O'Sullivan, *Our Burning Time* (Prometheus Books, 1965); *Revenants* (Prometheus Books, 1969).

Gloria Rawlinson, *The Islands Where I was Born* (Handcraft Press, 1955); *Of Clouds and Pebbles* (Paul's Book Arcade, 1963).

Keith Sinclair, *Songs for a Summer* (Pegasus Press, 1952); *A Time to Embrace* (Paul's Book Arcade, 1963).

Kendrick Smithyman, *The Blind Mountain* (Caxton Press, 1950); *The Penguin Book of New Zealand Verse* (Penguin, 1960, and Longman Paul, 1967); *Inheritance* (Paul's Book Arcade, 1962); *The New Zealand Listener* (vol. 59, 1968, and the Author).

Charles Spear, *Twopence Coloured* (Caxton Press, 1951).

C. K. Stead, *Whether the Will is Free* (Paul's Book Arcade, 1964).

Edward Tregear, *Shadows and Other Verses* (Whitcombe & Tombs, 1919).

Hone Tuwhare, *No Ordinary Sun* (Blackwood & Janet Paul, 1965); *Review '69* (Otago University Students' Association).

Raymond Ward, *Settler and Stranger* (Caxton Press, 1965).

Pat Wilson, *The Bright Sea* (Pegasus Press, 1951).

Hubert Witheford, *Shadow of the Flame, Poems 1942–7* (Pelorus Press, 1950); *The Lightning Makes a Difference* (Brookside Press, 1962, and the Author); *A Native, Perhaps Beautiful* (Caxton Press, 1967).

A few poems have been revised by their authors for this collection.

Mr. Packer's permission could not be obtained to reprint his poems.

INTRODUCTION

A NEW anthology of New Zealand poetry demands a clear-cut choice. Should its editor select a body of verse on lines that follow the contours of the country's development, the kind of collection that also provides material for the sociologist and historian, or one where each poem is included simply because it seems good poetry?

This selection is very much the second.

I have tried to represent each poet by a selection large enough to suggest his range in theme, and the variety of his form. There are some poets who have written their finest work in a short space of time, and I have made no attempt to spread their representation wider. With poets such as Curnow and Brasch a wide selection is still limiting. Other poets have put into a few poems all that is valuable in their work. A few may have just begun.

I do not believe that any anthology selected while three-quarters of its poets are still living, and while many of those are comparatively young, can claim any kind of finality. I prefer to regard this volume as a considered report on how New Zealand poetry stands now, and how it appears, looking back, from the end of the 1960s.

I

There were scores of colonists who published verse in the nineteenth century. They wrote poems which made New Zealand exotic, and poems which said how different from home. Yet as long as these things could be said, there was little more than physical conflict between man and environment. It was easy to acknowledge certain obvious contrasts between home and colony. One could enjoy nostalgia for one hemisphere, fascination with another. There was little tension, little uneasiness, that filtered through to poetry. Only seldom did a poem such as Edward Tregear's 'Te Whetu Plains' break through to a response that owed more to the awareness of an individual mind than to what currently was thought poetry's due. The apprehension of 'such ghastly peace', in a land for the most part too strange even to be misunderstood in a meaningful way, must have been a not uncommon feeling in colonial life. It is almost unique as it appears in verse.

Something inherent in the average British mind, once removed from home, and the tedium of a diction that was thought appropriate only to verse, continue to make the reading of nineteenth-century New Zealand verse an imposition. The landscape itself could be appreciated as the work of God, and a happy consequence of colonial policy. But chauvinism and evangelism stood between European and Maori before land disputes, the clamour for quick returns, and incomprehension hardened into war. Nothing in education or contemporary literature could prepare men to see their new country on any terms but their own, or with sensibilities uncluttered by what may have been relevant no longer.

Alfred Domett was the most ambitious of the colony's poets, and the man whose gifts were large enough to suffer the most. His *Ranolf and Amohia*, outrunning *Paradise Lost* in the number of its lines, drew from the Poet Laureate in 1872 the appraisal that he 'but wants limitation to be a very considerable poet'. That long idyllic epic, heavy with philosophy and erudition, is of some historical interest; but the poem had no machinery for experience, and remains a museum piece. The language had little in common with language used for anything else. Maoris remain the children of Rousseau, having nothing to do with the severity of Domett's racial views in parliament and press.

One feels that Tennyson's 'Enoch Arden' must acknowledge paternity for a great deal of bad verse where homesickness and a superficial exoticism were the areas attended. Such rhymes were the work of those who had crossed the world. The feeling of alienation, when it comes, is a more indigenous thing. It begins when what went before is not remembered at all, or is recalled through a sentimentality that sees things as they never were. When only hearsay, or reading, or a brief voyage of homage, is set against what is continually before one's eyes, reality is no longer exotic. It is all we have.

At this point there begins what one may call the colonial neurosis—regret for what one has not had, and yet an obsession with it; self-consciousness about what is one's own, and cannot be given. This leads to that most typical paradox: gaucherie and local assertiveness, on the one hand, and on the other, the rabid support of imperialism caught in Allen Curnow's line 'Seddon howling empire from an empty coast'.

The problem—one which a certain kind of New Zealander has never solved—was where to draw the line between those Englishmen who settled overseas, and those born overseas who claimed they were Englishmen. Many of the poems in this country's first anthology, Alexander and Currie's *New Zealand Verse* in 1906, insist on a vision that now seems as false to one country as it is to another. The England celebrated in 'an English lane, Where the primrose patches blow', is not the England many settlers, or their parents, had left behind them. Nor is the New Zealand where 'honey-loving wild birds kiss The kowhai's cups of gold' the land they came to, or were reared in. With the exception of Blanche Baughan, no poet before the First World War looked squarely at what was done, thought, and felt, in the full context of colonial or early Dominion life.

II

The first poets who almost consistently wrote well were R. A. K. Mason, who was born and educated in Auckland, and the older Englishwoman, Ursula Bethell. Neither paid service to predetermined diction or theme. They made it clear that a more rigorous use of language precludes, as a matter of course, what is second-hand in response.

Ursula Bethell is at her weakest when her voice is raised for public or traditional statement. When her poems begin at her fingertips, among her plants and shrubs, they ring most true.

That garden in the Cashmere Hills in Christchurch is not simply an extension of an English personality. It declares the uneasy truce between beauty watched over and cultivated, and the raw push of the seasons that offered Ursula Bethell involvement at the centre of growth, change, decline.

Tutored by the classics, and without Bethell's trust in natural beneficence, Mason often did not enjoy what he saw, but recorded the sight with extraordinary honesty and skill. It is no literary cliché to compare Mason's response to life with Thomas Hardy's. The same harshness informs them both, and a sympathy too profound to settle for any but the details of truth. A human Christ, and his extension in the lost, the betrayed, the intellectually honest, stands at the centre of Mason's refusal to concede comfort on the strength of hoping for it. Myth may have tailed off in the new world, yet the repetition of circumstances again initiates its relevance. What is biblical, what antipodean, in Christ on the swag, or in Judas that 'most sporting bird', are not questions we need to ask.

Eileen Duggan's was an equally honest mind, but one whose poems were muted by convention. Yet from a Georgian and Celtic inheritance she evolved, in a number of poems, and over many years, a hard-edged lyricism. At her best she brought a tougher grain to the tradition she had served.

The early 1930s saw a fresh excitement among students and younger writers. New Zealand, like everywhere else, was touched by the literary events of the decade before. A number of young men were to look at writing more critically, at their country less complacently.

As New Zealand approached its official centenary, Allen Curnow's was the voice to take up the complexities of a people for whom history continued to hold more reserved decisions than it did certainties. Curnow was fortunate in having Mason as an elder, and was gifted with linguistic and rhythmic resources of a high order. He turned to his country's past with a feeling of entailed involvement; to its present with the conviction— at times begrudged—that his reality as a man was here, or not at all.

The guilt that comes with a coastline appropriated through bloodshed, and the discovery that what these islands held out was 'something different, something Nobody counted on', are central to a myth, and to a corpus of verse, more compelling than anything else we have. Curnow's persistence in tracking New Zealand reality to its particulars, contracted in his later work to what lay within a man's own grasp, what passed before his eyes. It is as though reality, once assured in a broader context, must submit, step by step, until nervous responses, memory, and habit have been tested, and found not wanting.

The 1930s hold the beginnings of much else that we cannot now imagine ourselves without. A. R. D. Fairburn's output in poetry, satire, and occasional prose bear witness to a many-sided mind. He wrote more extensive political verse than did any other New Zealander. He castigated the society he lived in, yet his commitment was such that criticism at times brought him close to the elegiac. He saw in a decent regard for nature the basis of a finer national life. And when he confined himself to where his truest gift lay, he wrote from his preoccupation with love and death lyrics like 'Tapu' and 'The Cave'.

Denis Glover shared Fairburn's penchant for satire, and an eye acutely focused on what surrounded him. In the early 1950s he was to find, in sequences grouped about the legendary figures of gold-digger and solitary, a form superbly fitted to his spare, lyrical voice. Nowhere else do the land's lock upon mind and body, and the liberation possible within its bond, work so memorably into poetry.

In Charles Brasch natural beauty frequently becomes a touchstone for what man has not lived up to in his uneasy tenure. Brasch's verse is thoughtfully wrought and for the most part meagre in metaphor. In five volumes, over thirty years, he has asked, and suggested, where in the intricacies of history and time, human values reside. More recently, his poetry has sought to build, from what the emotions have verified, a bulwark that at least ensures breathing space in a world where questions, if put at all, seldom can be put with expectation of reply.

A man who lives in this country today does not generally have to come to terms with the land. For better or worse, that land, for the time being, offers those who live with her too comfortable a life to talk of hostility. There is still hard physical work, but there is little feeling of a battle to be won, unless self-imposed by mountaineering, the vagaries of the sea, or the choice of back-country jobs. Not man and the land, but man in a welfare state society, man in love, man in the flow of a larger world around him, are the concerns of most of our poets since 1950. The look of New Zealand, the feel of it, must continue to furnish the staple of much impulse, to serve as the mould where much feeling settles most effectively. To go that one step farther, and claim that only in what is recognizably New Zealand can valid poetry begin, has come to be more than a little narcissistic.

It is self-definition that occupies the greater part of our poetry. To harden this into defining national consciousness, along particular lines, now seems too crude. Often critical insistence presses on the supposed common experience of being a New Zealander, and on the demand for evidence in a poem that is consistent with it. This is trying to wring community statement from a number of individual necks. There is not much that could be called a cultural inheritance in the New Zealand pakeha way of life. There is no folk-tradition, and there are aspects of life in these islands that no writer, in verse or prose, has yet touched on. What we have to look to are a number of fine individuals, in writing, painting, and music. The sum to which such individuals tend, a distinct quality of life, cannot be presumed.

I take at random four of the poets represented in this collection. The grandparents of the first were Jewish, and settled in the South Island. The second, whose father was Scottish and mother Polynesian, has lived the greater part of his life in Wellington. The third's grandparents came from Sweden on one side, his great-grandparents from Ireland on the other, and the family was settled in the Waikato. The fourth, who now lives in England, had English forebears, and grew up on the east coast of the North

Island. To try to find points of similarity between these men is difficult. To elicit from their poems, from their imagery or language or themes, something of which we can say 'yes, this is New Zealand, and what we value', seems not so much impossible as to direct attention falsely. It is possible that some racial inheritance, some detail from mythology or folk-lore unknown to the majority of his countrymen, just as some half-remembered incident from childhood, or by-way of education, may be central to each poet. These materials may be of far greater importance to poetry than what he has looked at often, what he has read in other poems, or what touches his life from day to day.

Glover, Baxter, Campbell, to select names at random, are three fine poets. Try to link them through some thread of imagery, some common areas of interest, in the cause of national consciousness, and each poet is diminished. To go further, and say that in certain elements of each, one detects the flow of a 'tradition', is not to concern ourselves with what is valued most in each man's work.

IV

Charles Spear's one small volume, *Twopence Coloured*, was published in 1951. Spear, who grants little to metrical innovations, and uses language with *fin-de-siècle* preciousness, is modern for more than his wry distortions, or the panoply of erudition ironically trifled with. He persuades us to accept seriously a contemporary tone that penetrates his unaccommodating form and diction. The reality of detail, the relevance of mood, survive among the slanted mirrors of fairy-tale, historical snippet, and pose. In the minute clarity of a glass-paperweight world, feeling evokes a strange wasteland, a fantasy that one accepts as life. Only he and M. K. Joseph can so lightly employ learning, touch deeply with it, and lay claim to overtly scholarly verse.

Kendrick Smithyman emerged as a writer at much the same time. He is capable of more genuinely complex verse than any of his contemporaries. Almost as often, he continues to publish poems that seem unrewardingly obscure, where even syntax is

xxv

not assured safe conduct. Yet there is a considerable *œuvre* of dexterity and wit, which examines man in terms of the places and activities he is most at ease with, or works the kind of myth sustained in 'Parable of Two Talents'.

A good deal of our prose has insisted that New Zealand life has little emotional resonance. Because of society's disparateness, its divided ambitions, its inability in recent years to define with much enthusiasm or precision what those ambitions are, social verse has vast tracts to exercise it. In the wake of the failed socialist dream, the years from 1950 have less optimism to show on many levels than the preceding twenty.

Louis Johnson is the most consistent in the attention he directs to the hollowness of our social life, and regret for what it stifles. A large part of James K. Baxter's work shares the same concern. But Johnson's values, when they can be detected, are humanist. Baxter draws on another view of man which a histrionic Catholicism cannot altogether obscure. His morality is a Hebraic wolf in New Testament fleeces. The fall of man, emotionally, takes precedence over the efficacy of grace. Baxter's increasing tendency—particularly in his several plays—is to locate value only in the social outcast, the habitual sinner. God's justice has further to relent, his mercy more to redeem. The poet does, of course, go beyond the limits of his theology. He is capable of uncovering areas of response, and embodying them in poems of such formal rhetorical skill, that no other New Zealand poet can keep him company. Baxter's ballads, far from his least achievements, bring poetry closer to the language and conceptions of the people he writes of than has been common with our verse. They are among that very small body of New Zealand poetry of which it makes sense to say that it speaks for a community, and is literary work.

It is ironical that at a time when so many writers have misgivings at their country's increasing dependence on the United States, American poetry is the strongest influence on our recent verse. There is no reason to expect that this will change while Americans continue to write so much that is among the best. Although Gloria Rawlinson has written a fine sequence about childhood in Tonga, no European New Zealand poet has drawn successfully on Polynesian poetry or lore. (This, of course, does not apply to much of Campbell's work, nor to all of Tuwhare's. In different ways, they *are* that tradition. There is no question of their merely deriving from it.) And those poems of Robin Hyde's that found so much of value in China are now thirty years old, and remain all that has come from contact with Asia.

Poetry here, as elsewhere, recently has tended away from public statement, or from too loud a declaration of beliefs. Anything that passes as large political comment has attracted little literary talent. Apart from well-established names such as Baxter, Smithyman, and Campbell, one now looks to strong, personal work like Fleur Adcock's; to Gordon Challis's quasi-scientific gutting of neuroses; to Hubert Witheford's singular precision in his continual whittling of language; or to poems like K. O. Arvidson's declension of a symbol, in 'Fish and Chips on the Merry-go-round', to register an amused distaste at the way ideals turn out. In Michael Jackson's African poems, or Owen Leeming's 'Priests of Serrabonne', one sees most clearly the open-ended range of current verse.

V

Europe is the closest that a New Zealander has to an extensive birthright. How each poet goes about constructing for himself a coherent body of verse, aware that geography and history have deprived him of much that is valuable, even as they give what cannot be done without, is of permanent interest in New Zealand verse. And what at first appears to be a cultural penalty may in fact be construed as rigorous liberty.

A poet anywhere is free to adapt from what has been central, or peripheral, to his tradition. In a milieu with not only fewer of the usual pressures, but the actual absence of such pressures at work upon him, even a very minor poet may find that simply to adapt is to construct. It is to do, in the poetry that springs from the men with whom he shares time and place, something that may not have been done before, or not done in such a way as to mean the same thing. This constant relation to poetry written in English, anywhere, as well as to the poetry of his own countrymen, does not, except for a particular mind that would be patriotic even in this, involve double standards. It is only by accepting each as naturally one's own that richness and uniqueness evolve. It offers a double interest which is far from the least excitement of New Zealand poetry.

EDWARD TREGEAR

Te Whetu Plains

A lonely rock above a midnight plain,
 A sky across whose moonlit darkness flies
No shadow from the 'Children of the Rain',
 A stream whose double crescent far-off lies,
 And seems to glitter back the silver of the skies.

The table-lands stretch step by step below
 In giant terraces, their deeper ledges
Banded by blackened swamps (that, near, I know
 Convolvulus-entwined) whose whitened edges
 Are ghostly silken flags of seeding water-sedges.

All still, all silent, 'tis a songless land,
 That hears no music of the nightingale,
No sound of waters falling lone and grand
 Through sighing forests to the lower vale,
 No whisper in the grass, so wan, and grey, and pale.

When Earth was tottering in its infancy,
 This rock, a drop of molten stone, was hurled
And tost on waves of flames like those we see
 (Distinctly though afar) evolved and whirled
 A photosphere of fire around the Solar World.

Swift from the central deeps the lightning flew
 Piercing the heart of Darkness like a spear,
Hot blasts of steam and vapour thunder'd through
 The lurid blackness of the atmosphere.
 A million years have passed, and left strange quiet here.

Peace, the deep peace of universal death
 Enshrouds the kindly mother-earth of old,

The air is dead, and stirs no living breath
    To break these awful Silences that hold
    The heart within their clutch, and numb the veins with
        cold.

My soul hath wept for Rest with longing tears,
    Called it 'the perfect crown of human life'—
But now I shudder lest the coming years
    Should be with these most gloomy terrors rife;
    When palsied arms drop down outwearied with the strife.

May Age conduct me by a gentle hand
    Beneath the shadows ever brooding o'er
The solemn twilight of the Evening Land,
    Where man's discordant voices pierce no more,
    But sleeping waters dream along a sleeping shore.

Where I, when Youth has spent its fiery strength
    And flickers low, may rest in quietness
Till on my waiting brow there falls at length
    The deeper calm of the Death-Angel's kiss—
    But not, oh God, such peace, such ghastly peace as this.

B. E. BAUGHAN

The Old Place
New Zealand

So the last day's come at last, the close of my fifteen year—
The end of the hope, an' the struggles, an' messes I've put in
here.
All of the shearings over, the final mustering done,—
Eleven hundred an' fifty for the incoming man, near on.
Over five thousand I drove 'em, mob by mob, down the coast;
Eleven-fifty in fifteen year . . . it isn't much of a boast.

Oh, it's a bad old place! Blown out o' your bed half the nights,
And in summer the grass burnt shiny an' bare as your hand, on
the heights:
The creek dried up by November, and in May a thundering roar
That carries down toll o' your stock to salt 'em whole on the
shore.
Clear'd I have, and I've clear'd an' clear'd, yet everywhere, slap
in your face,
Briar, tauhinu, an' ruin!—God! it's a brute of a place.
. . . An' the house got burnt which I built, myself, with all that
worry and pride;
Where the Missus was always homesick, and where she took
fever, and died.

Yes, well! I'm leaving the place. Apples look red on that
bough.
I set the slips with my own hand. Well—they're the other man's
now.
The breezy bluff: an' the clover that smells so over the land,
Drowning the reek o' the rubbish, that plucks the profit out o'
your hand:
That bit o' Bush paddock I fall'd myself, an' watch'd, each year,
come clean

3

(Don't it look fresh in the tawny? A scrap of Old-Country
    green):
This air, all healthy with sun an' salt, an' bright with purity:
An' the glossy karakas there, twinkling to the big blue twinkling
    sea:
Ay, the broad blue sea beyond, an' the gem-clear cove below,
Where the boat I'll never handle again, sits rocking to and fro:
There's the last look to it all! an' now for the last upon
This room, where Hetty was born, an' my Mary died, an'
    John . . .
Well! I'm leaving the poor old place, and it cuts as keen as a
    knife;
The place that's broken my heart—the place where I've lived
    my life.

from *A Bush Section*

Logs, at the door, by the fence; logs, broadcast over the paddock;
Sprawling in motionless thousands away down the green of the
    gully,
Logs, grey-black. And the opposite rampart of ridges
Bristles against the sky, all the tawny, tumultuous landscape
Is stuck, and prickled, and spiked with the standing black and
    grey splinters,
Strewn, all over its hollows and hills, with the long, prone, grey-
    black logs.

    For along the paddock, and down the gully,
    Over the multitudinous ridges,
    Through valley and spur,
    Fire has been!
Ay, the Fire went through and the Bush has departed,
The green Bush departed, green Clearing is not yet come.
    'Tis a silent, skeleton world;
    Dead, and not yet re-born,

4

Made, unmade, and scarcely as yet in the making;
Ruin'd, forlorn, and blank.

*　　　*　　　*

Day after day,
The hills stand out on the sky,
The splinters stand on the hills,
In the paddock the logs lie prone.
The prone logs never arise,
The erect ones never grow green,
Leaves never rustle, the birds went away with the Bush,—
There is no change, nothing stirs!
And tonight there is no change;
All is mute, monotonous, stark;
In the whole wide sweep round the low little hut of the settler
No life to be seen; nothing stirs.

*　　　*　　　*

. . . It is stiller than ever; the wind has fallen.
The moist air brings,
To mix with the spicy breath of the young break-wind macro-
　　carpa,
Wafts of the acrid, familiar aroma of slowly-smouldering logs.
And, hark, through the empty silence and dimness
Solemnly clear,
Comes the wistful, haunting cry of some lonely, far-away
　　morepork,
'*Kia toa!* Be brave!'
—Night is come.
Now the gully is hidden, the logs and the paddock all hidden.
Brightly the Stars shine out! . . .
The sky is a wide black paddock, without any fences,
The Stars are its shining logs;
Here, sparse and single, but yonder, as logg'd-up for burning,
Close in a cluster of light.
And the thin clouds, they are the hills,
They are the spurs of the heavens,
On whose steepnesses scatter'd, the Star-logs silently lie:

Dimm'd as it were by the distance, or maybe in mists of the mountain
Tangled—yet still they brighten, not darken, the thick-strewn slopes!
But see! these hills of the sky
They waver and move! their gullies are drifting, and driving;
Their ridges, uprooted,
Break, wander and flee, they escape! casting careless behind them
Their burdens of brightness, the Stars, that rooted remain.
—No! they do not remain. No! even they cannot be steadfast.
For the curv'd Three (that yonder
So glitter and sparkle
There, over the bails),
This morning, at dawn,
At the start of the milking,
Stood pale on the brink of yon rocky-ledged hill;
And the Cross, o'er the viaduct
Now, then was slanting,
Almost to vanishing, over the snow.
So, the Stars travel, also?
The poor earthly logs, in the wan earthly paddocks,
Never can move, they must stay;
But over the heavenly pastures, the bright, live logs of the heavens
Wander at will, looking down on our paddocks and logs, and pass on.
'O friendly and beautiful Live-Ones!
Coming to us for a little,
Then travelling and passing, while here with our logs we remain,
What are you? Where do you come from?
Who are you? Where do you go?'

*   *   *

O pioneer Soul! against Ruin here hardily pitted,
What life wilt thou make of existence?
Life! what more Life wilt thou make?

*   *   *

6

Here in the night, face to face
With the Burnt Bush within and without thee,
Standing, small and alone:
Bright Promise on Poverty's threshold!
      What art thou? Where hast thou come from?
      How far, how far! wilt thou go?

ARTHUR H. ADAMS

The Dwellings of our Dead

They lie unwatched, in waste and vacant places,
In sombre bush or wind-swept tussock spaces,
   Where seldom human tread
And never human trace is—
   The dwellings of our dead!

No insolence of stone is o'er them builded;
By mockery of monuments unshielded,
   Far on the unfenced plain
Forgotten graves have yielded
   Earth to free earth again.

Above their crypts no air with incense reeling,
No chant of choir or sob of organ pealing;
   But ever over them
The evening breezes kneeling
   Whisper a requiem.

For some the margeless plain where no one passes,
Save when at morning far in misty masses
   The drifting flock appears.
Lo, here the greener grasses
   Glint like a stain of tears!

For some the quiet bush, shade-strewn and saddened,
Whereo'er the herald tui, morning-gladdened,
   Lone on his chosen tree,
With his new rapture maddened,
   Shouts incoherently.

For some the gully, where in whispers tender,
The flax-blades mourn and murmur, and the slender
   White ranks of toi go,

With drooping plumes of splendour,
  In pageantry of woe.

For some the common trench where, not all fameless,
They fighting fell who thought to tame the tameless,
  And won their barren crown;
Where one grave holds them nameless—
  Brave white and braver brown.

But in their sleep, like troubled children turning,
A dream of mother-country in them burning,
  They whisper their despair,
And one vague, voiceless yearning
  Burdens the pausing air . . .

'Unchanging here the drab year onward presses;
No Spring comes trysting here with new-loosed tresses,
  And never may the years
Win Autumn's sweet caresses—
  Her leaves that fall like tears.

And we would lie 'neath old-remembered beeches,
Where we could hear the voice of him who preaches
  And the deep organ's call,
While close about us reaches
  The cool, grey, lichened wall.'

But they are ours, and jealously we hold them;
Within our children's ranks we have enrolled them,
  And till all Time shall cease
Our brooding bush shall fold them
  In her broad-bosomed peace.

They came as lovers come, all else forsaking,
The bonds of home and kindred proudly breaking;
  They lie in splendour lone—
The nation of their making
  Their everlasting throne!

9

MARY URSULA BETHELL

Response

When you wrote your letter it was April,
And you were glad that it was spring weather,
And that the sun shone out in turn with showers of rain.

I write in waning May and it is autumn,
And I am glad that my chrysanthemums
Are tied up fast to strong posts,
So that the south winds cannot beat them down.
I am glad that they are tawny coloured,
And fiery in the low west evening light.
And I am glad that one bush warbler
Still sings in the honey-scented wattle . . .

But oh, we have remembering hearts,
And we say 'How green it was in such and such an April',
And 'Such and such an autumn was very golden',
And 'Everything is for a very short time'.

Pause

When I am very earnestly digging
I lift my head sometimes, and look at the mountains,
And muse upon them, muscles relaxing.

I think how freely the wild grasses flower there,
How grandly the storm-shaped trees are massed in their gorges
And the rain-worn rocks strewn in magnificent heaps.

Pioneer plants on those uplands find their own footing;
No vigorous growth, there, is an evil weed:
All weathers are salutary.

It is only a little while since this hillside
Lay untrammelled likewise,
Unceasingly swept by transmarine winds.

In a very little while, it may be,
When our impulsive limbs and our superior skulls
Have to the soil restored several ounces of fertilizer,

The Mother of all will take charge again,
And soon wipe away with her elements
Our small fond human enclosures.

Detail

My garage is a structure of excessive plainness,
It springs from a dry bank in the back garden,
It is made of corrugated iron,
And painted all over with brick-red.

But beside it I have planted a green Bay-tree,
—A sweet Bay, an Olive, and a Turkey Fig,
—A Fig, an Olive, and a Bay.

Soothsayer

I walked about the garden in the evening,
And thought: How Autumn lingers—
Still a few gold chrysanthemums—
Still one late rose—
The old blackbird still has voice.

I walked back down the pathway,
The evening light lay gently on the orchard;
Then I saw a redness on the peach boughs,
And bulb-spears pushing upwards,

And heard the old blackbird whistle—
'Get ready. Get ready. Get ready.
Quick. Quick. Spring.'

So I cut down the last chrysanthemums,
Pulled up their stakes and piled them in the shed,
At hand to serve me soon for young delphiniums.

Erica

Sit down with me awhile beside the heath-corner.

Here have I laboured hour on hour in winter,
Digging thick clay, breaking up clods, and draining,
Carrying away cold mud, bringing up sandy loam,
Bringing these rocks and setting them all in their places,
To be shelter from winds, shade from too burning sun.

See, now, how sweetly all these plants are springing
Green, ever green, and flowering turn by turn,
Delicate heaths, and their fragrant Australian kinsmen,
Shedding, as once unknown in New Holland, strange scents
    on the air,
And purple and white daboecia—the Irish heather—
Said in the nurseryman's list to be so well suited
For small gardens, for rock gardens, and for graveyards.

Fall

Autumn, I think, now.

Rose hues assume a deeper intensity.
Little birds flying in from far in the wild bush
Pursue insects boldly even into our parlours.

The play of the winds is less turbulent:
They scatter gently forspent petallage,
And a scent of ripe seeds is borne on their soft gusts.

Today I do not perceive the outcry of young folk;
Perhaps they are helping to get in some harvest,
Or far afield for important ball-games.

Only old men pause by the sunny roadside
Noticing the same sights that I have noticed,
And listening to the same quietness.

We do not regret that we are of ripe years;
We do not complain of grey hairs and infirmities;
We are drowsy and very ready to fall into deep sleep.

Trance

While others slept I rose, and looked upon the garden,
Lying so still there in the rare light of the soon-to-be-setting moon.

The soft, sharp shadows marked a familiar pattern,
But not a leaf stirred, not a blade of grass quivered,
The trees seemed petrified, and the hedges cut out of black glass.

So still it lay, it suffered an enchantment.
It was the dimly mirrored image of a grove laid up in heaven,
Or the calm mirage of a long-since-lost oasis,
Or the unflickering dream of a serene midnight
Dreamt by one falling into profound sleep.

It was the spectral vision of a work accomplished, done with.
Veiled in the silvery mists of very long past years;
Myself the wraith, from all vicissitude abstracted,
Of one who had, perhaps, once known expectance,
Had sown in tears and learnt the grave joys of harvest,
Had long ago, perhaps, an enclosed garden tended,
Had for a short while, perhaps, been happy there.

The Long Harbour

There are three valleys where the warm sun lingers,
gathered to a green hill girt-about anchorage,
and gently, gently, at the cobbled margin
of fire-formed, time-smoothed, ocean-moulded curvature,
a spent tide fingers the graven boulders,
the black, sea-bevelled stones.

The fugitive hours, in those sun-loved valleys,
implacable hours, their golden-wheeled chariots'
inaudible passage check, and slacken
their restless teams' perpetual galloping;
and browsing, peaceable sheep and cattle
gaze as they pause by the way.

Grass springs sweet where once thick forest
gripped vales by fire and axe freed to pasturage;
but flame and blade have spared the folding gullies,
and there, still, the shade-flitting, honey-sipping lutanists
copy the dropping of tree-cool waters
dripping from stone to stone.

White hawthorn hedge from old, remembered England,
and orchard white, and whiter bridal clematis
the bush-bequeathed, conspire to strew the valleys
in tender spring, and blackbird, happy colonist,
and blacker, sweeter-fluted tui echo
either the other's song.

From far, palm-feathery, ocean-spattered islands
there rowed hither dark and daring voyagers;
and Norseman, Gaul, the Briton and the German
sailed hither singing; all these hardy venturers
they desired a home, and have taken their rest there,
and their songs are lost on the wind.

I have walked here with my love in the early spring-time,
and under the summer-dark walnut-avenues,
and played with the children, and waited with the aged
by the quayside, and listened alone where manukas
sighing, windswept, and sea-answering pine-groves
garrison the burial-ground.

It should be very easy to lie down and sleep there
in that sequestered hillside ossuary,
underneath a billowy, sun-caressed grass-knoll,
beside those dauntless, tempest-braving ancestresses
who pillowed there so gladly, gnarled hands folded,
their tired, afore-translated bones.

It would not be a hard thing to wake up one morning
to the sound of bird-song in scarce-stirring willow-trees,
waves lapping, oars plashing, chains running slowly,
and faint voices calling across the harbour;
to embark at dawn, following the old forefathers,
to put forth at daybreak for some lovelier,
still undiscovered shore.

Warning of Winter

Give over, now, red roses;
Summer-long you told us,
Urgently unfolding, death-sweet, life-red,
Tidings of love. All's said. Give over.

Summer-long you placarded
Leafy shades with heart-red
Symbols. Who knew not love at first knows now,
Who had forgot has now remembered.

Let be, let be, lance-lilies,
Alert, pard-spotted, tilting

Poised anthers, flaming; have done flaming fierce;
Hard hearts were pierced long since, and stricken.

Give to the blast your thorn-crowns
Roses; and now be torn down
All you ardent lilies, your high-holden crests,
Havocked and cast to rest on the clammy ground.

Alas, alas, to darkness
Descends the flowered pathway,
To solitary places, deserts, utter night;
To issue in what hidden dawn of light hereafter?

But one, in dead of winter,
Divine *Agape*, kindles
Morning suns, new moons, lights starry trophies;
Says to the waste: Rejoice, and bring forth roses;
To the ice-fields: Let here spring thick bright lilies.

Decoration

This jar of roses and carnations on the window-sill,
Crimson upon sky-grey and snow-wrapt mountain-pallor,
(Sharp storm's asseveration of cold winter's on-coming,)
How strange their look, how lovely, rich and foreign,
The living symbol of a season put away.

A letter-sheaf, bound up by time-frayed filament,
I found; laid by; youth's flowering.
The exotic words blazed up blood-red against death's shadow,
Red upon grey. Red upon grey.

Midnight

All day long, prismatic dazzle,
Clashing of musics, challenge, encounter, succession;
Gear-change on the up-and-down hill of hypothesis;
Choice, choice, decision, events rivetting shackles;
Hazardous tests, new wine of escape . . .
        oh, strange noviciate!
Bright stimulus, venture, tension, poised preparedness.

But at midnight, infinite darkness,
Opulent silence, liberty, liberty, solitude;
The acrid, mountainy wind's austere caresses;
Rest, rest, compensation, very suspension of death;
Deep stillness of death, dark negation . . .
        ah, thy heart-beat,
Origin, Signification, dread Daysman, Consummator.

Lever de Rideau

Today
the clocks strike
seven, seven, seven, and church-bells
chime busily, and the plain-town heavily wakes;
a salt-sharp east wind flicks and swells
and tosses my emerald silk curtains;
translucent green on blue the empyrean, and lo!
north and west, endlessly limned and painted,
my mountains, my mountains, all snow.

Now a change begins in the heavenly tone-chord;
to the east, eyes! where the sea is incised
like azure ice on sky of vermeil;
oh, dream on prolonged, beautiful prelude!
hushed still, delay, summoning bird-song!
hold, magic touch, be arrested, lovely crisis of sunrise!

17

when yonder death-white summits are rose-flushed
and glittering, I must
away.

October Morning

'All clear, all clear, all clear!' after the storm in the morning
The birds sing; all clear the rain-scourged firmament,
All clear the still blue horizontal sea;
And what, all white again? all white the long line of the
    mountains
And clear on sky's sheer blue intensity.

Gale raved night-long, but all clear, now, in the sunlight
And sharp, earth-scented air, a fair new day.
The jade and emerald squares of far-spread cultivated
All clear, and powdered foot-hills, snow-fed waterway,
And every black pattern of plantation made near;
All clear, the city set—but oh for taught interpreter,
To translate the quality, the excellence, for initiate seer
To tell the essence of this hallowed clarity,
Reveal the secret meaning of the symbol: 'clear'.

Evening Walk in Winter

Tussock burned to fine gold, and the sheep bore golden fleeces
by the sudden alchemy of wintry waning sun,
and stepping eastwards
My arrowy shadow sapphire led me on.

So airy light I seemed to climb, the earthy path so gilded,
the illumined hill appeared in that transmuted hour
olympian,
the self a quenchless effluence of fire.

But overhead marmoreal white now hung the cold moon ominous
in ashen blue of empty dome, our doom
exhibit thus
even so to frozen death we must all come.

Now lost the living orb, and all his spacious ardours
concealed behind black rocky alps in wintry grave.
Falling darkness
possessed the plain, pale streams, sad fields and groves.

Now stars rushed out to fill the void with sparkling affirmations,
their cold acumen spoke no comfort, as before,
the heavens vacant;
mirror-moon shone false from fire afar.

Darkly alone, the errant hour outspent, led downwards
by homing track, the lowly glittering chain
lit round
hearth-fastness beckoned there was warmth within.

Oh not by late-launched planets flung in heavens equivocal
may we, or making moonlight wan and wild
oracular,
be certified of life or death, of heat or cold.

The bright particular hearts mysteriously enkindled
for us—the daily love, like fire that glows and runs
half hidden
among the embers—this the warmth we live by, our unsetting sun.

What if the light go out? What if some black disaster
of total nightfall quench the vivid spark?
Oh might we hearken,
then, with night-initiate Spaniard to the Answerer
who said: I am the dark.

from *By the River Ashley*

VI

The hour is dark. The river comes to its end,
Comes to the embrace of the all enveloping sea.
My story comes to its end.

> Divine Picnicker by the lakeside,
> Familiar friend of the fishermen,
> Known and yet not known, lost and yet found,
> The hour is dark, come down to the riverside,
> The strange river, come find me.
> Bring if it might be companions
> In the tissue of the Kingdom, but come thou,
> Key to all mystery, opening and none shall shut again,
> Innermost love of all loves, making all one.
> Come.

The Man with the Wooden Leg

There was a man lived quite near us;
He had a wooden leg and a goldfinch in a green cage.
His name was Farkey Anderson,
And he'd been in a war to get his leg.
We were very sad about him,
Because he had such a beautiful smile
And was such a big man to live in a very small house.
When he walked on the road his leg did not matter so much;
But when he walked in his little house
It made an ugly noise.
Little Brother said his goldfinch sang the loudest of all birds,
So that he should not hear his poor leg
And feel too sorry about it.

Sanary

Her little hot room looked over the bay
Through a stiff palisade of glinting palms,
And there she would lie in the heat of the day,
Her dark head resting upon her arms,
So quiet, so still, she did not seem
To think, to feel, or even to dream.

The shimmering, blinding web of sea
Hung from the sky, and the spider sun
With busy frightening cruelty
Crawled over the sky and spun and spun.
She could see it still when she shut her eyes,
And the little boats caught in the web like flies.

Down below at this idle hour
Nobody walked in the dusty street

A scent of dying mimosa flower
Lay on the air, but sweet—too sweet.

To L. H. B.

Last night for the first time since you were dead
I walked with you, my brother, in a dream.
We were at home again beside the stream
Fringed with tall berry bushes, white and red.
'Don't touch them: they are poisonous,' I said.
But your hand hovered, and I saw a beam
Of strange, bright laughter flying round your head,
And as you stooped I saw the berries gleam.
'Don't you remember? We called them Dead Man's Bread!'
I woke and heard the wind moan and the roar
Of the dark water tumbling on the shore.
Where—where is the path of my dream for my eager feet?
By the remembered stream my brother stands
Waiting for me with berries in his hands . . .
'These are my body. Sister, take and eat.'

To Stanislaw Wyspianski[1]

From the other side of the world,
From a little island cradled in the giant sea bosom,
From a little land with no history,
(Making its own history, slowly and clumsily
Piecing together this and that, finding the pattern, solving the
    problem,
Like a child with a box of bricks),
I, a woman, with the taint of the pioneer in my blood,
Full of a youthful strength that wars with itself and is lawless,
I sing your praises, magnificent warrior; I proclaim your
    triumphant battle.
My people have had nought to contend with;

They have worked in the broad light of day and handled the clay
     with rude fingers;
Life—a thing of blood and muscle; Death—a shovelling under-
     ground of waste material.
What would they know of ghosts and unseen presences,
Of shadows that blot out reality, of darkness that stultifies morn?
Fine and sweet the water that runs from their mountains;
How could they know of poisonous weed, of rotted and clogging
     tendrils?
And the tapestry woven from dreams of your tragic childhood
They would tear in their stupid hands,
The sad, pale light of your soul blow out with their childish
     laughter.
But the dead—the old—Oh Master, we belong to you there;
Oh Master, there we are children and awed by the strength of a
     giant;
How alive you leapt into the grave and wrestled with Death
And found in the veins of Death the red blood flowing
And raised Death up in your arms and showed him to all the
     people.
Yours a more personal labour than the Nazarene's miracles,
Yours a more forceful encounter than the Nazarene's gentle
     commands.
Stanislaw Wyspianski—Oh man with the name of a fighter,
Across these thousands of sea-shattered miles we cry and proclaim
     you;
We say 'He is lying in Poland, and Poland thinks he is dead;
But he gave the denial to Death—he is lying there, wakeful;
The blood in his giant heart pulls red through his veins'.

[1] Stanislaw Wyspianski was born in the 1860s and died prematurely in 1907.
He was a dramatic poet and has been described as the greatest literary genius
produced by modern Poland. The keynote of his work is an unconquerable faith
in the future of his country.

J. R. HERVEY

Somnambulist

He could not fall so far,
Nor ever be so lost in a murmuration
Of dreams as not to lie
Still on the startled path of evocation.

Whose voice was it that scattered
The deep defence of sleep, that flattered
The dubious brain into escapade?

It was the frigid hour of resurrection
When he arose, and night drew back
From the body that slid from all correction,
Whose implacable face
Knew the blotted road and the empty appointed place.

Two Old Men Look at the Sea

They do not speak but into their empty mood
    Receive the leaden utterance of waves,
    And intimations blowing from old graves,
    Men who have already crossed to the torpid sandspit
    Between life and death, whose cold rejected hands
    Have flung farewell to passion, the brassy lands
    Of love and pursuit, who even taste not life
    In the pomp of passing synopsis, but only savour
    The salty wind and sand swirling up to claim
    The total mystery masking in a name.

How shall we live and hold, how love and handle
    To the last beach the dark and difficult gleanings?
    For so must we come, hugging our recompense,
    To the unfeeling shore, to the bleak admonitory tide,

Our fear being as a hand that cups a candle
Against the winds that whiff away pretence,
And the sea whose sentence strikes like a leaden wave.

Man on a Raft

Not out of the war, not out of the agitated
House of life and wearing the brand of love,
He is yet no more than the diving bird between
    Wave and wave.

Only one is near, only one regards, death,
In the stare of the sky, in the cold watch of water:
And who but death trundles the eccentric toy,
    The dancing timber.

But always he skirted the vortex of disaster,
For the crazy earth carried him and lost him
Among the witless stars and hostile calms,
    Smothering knowledge.

His days have sickened in the heavy perfume
Of death hanging a flower on every season:
His hope has stumbled over crooked stones,
    Pretending sleep.

Where shall be his landfall who resigns
The rudder, whose hands, twin-gods of design,
Are but fists that threaten doom and beat like flowers
    On the iron doors?

Yet the rag at the mast was valid, it persuaded
The clean prow of love, and the man on the raft
Climbed to the assured deck, the rational voyage,
    Drowning fear.

The Empty Valley

Yeats could not walk in the disarming field without
Feeling at elbow spirit or devil,
Nor hear an idle shout
But he proclaimed a shred of ghostly revel.

If but the countryman, he said,
Had the keen ear and eagle sight
Of Swedenborg he would hear the noise
Of swords in the empty valley—shall we go at the side
Of the poet and mingle
With marches of spirit or stand
With the countryman who sees as single
The abundant land?

This beauty shall be my love, I shall not ask
If nature be an ineffectual mask
Through which death-chastened eyes
Persuade the wise,

I shall not look to left or right
For a cold companion nor suspect the night,
Nor regard the rally
Of irrelevant swords—
What so replete as the empty valley?

Children Among the Tombstones

The O so gay
Among the text-strewn graves at play—
Says nothing the heaven-telling story
To inmates of the earlier glory.

Mourning the wrangle
Between life and death a carven angel—

Too near the beginning to see the end
They danced with time the trumped up friend.

And sprinkled over
With loves and flowers and songs to cover
From ghosts and stones so down to death,
And mounded hints that hold their breath.

To party laughs
They could invite the epitaphs,
Wiseacre text and monument—
No death, no death, the word was sent.

From the wide eyed
Of world without end was nothing to hide,
Necropolis nurse of endless play,
No death, no death whistled the day.

EILEEN DUGGAN

Booty

Ah not as plains that spread into us slowly
But as that mountain flinging at the skies
And not as merchantmen which trundle in the offing
But as a privateer that boards a prize,
Let song come always at me and not to me
And, coming, let it plunder, burn, and flay,
For beauty like heaven by violence is taken
And the violent shall bear it away.

Pilgrimage

Now are the bells unlimbered from their spires
In every steeple-loft from pole to pole:
The four winds wheel and blow into this gate,
And every wind is wet with carillons.
And two Americas at eagle-height,
The pure, abstracted Himalayan chimes,
Great ghosts of clappers from the Russian fries,
And sweet, wind-sextoned tremblers from Cathay;
The bells of Ireland, jesting all the way,
The English bells, slowbosomed as a swan,
The queenly, weary din of Notre Dame,
And the Low Countries ringing back the sea.
Then Spain, the Moor still moaning through the saint,
The frosty, fiery bells of Germany,
And on before them, baying, sweeping down,
The heavy, joyful pack of thunder-jowls
That tongue hosannas from the leash of Rome—
All float untethered over Jaffa Gate
To fling one peal when angels cheat the stone.
But if one little gaping country bell,
Blown from its weather-boarding in the south,

Should be too lost to keep its covenant,
Or lift its heart and reins up to the hour,
Know that its dumbness riots more than sound.

The Tides Run up the Wairau

The tides run up the Wairau
That fights against their flow.
My heart and it together
Are running salt and snow.

For though I cannot love you,
Yet, heavy, deep, and far,
Your tide of love comes swinging,
Too swift for me to bar.

Some thought of you must linger,
A salt of pain in me,
For oh what running river
Can stand against the sea?

The Bushfeller

Lord, mind your trees today!
My man is out there clearing.
God send the chips fly safe.
My heart is always fearing.

And let the axehead hold!
My dreams are all of felling.
He earns our bread far back.
And then there is no telling.

If he came home at nights,
We'd know, but it is only—

We might not even hear--
A man could lie there lonely.

God, let the trunks fall clear,
He did not choose his calling;
He's young and full of life—
A tree is heavy, falling.

Have No Fear!

In any element, you are scot-free.
Whatever faction triumphs you are safe.
Matching its medium,
What is abeyant
Assumes responsibility.
The switch from gill to lung
To you is nothing.
Behold the complete axolotl!
And should, as some say,
The world end by fire,
You, a salamandrine,
Would usurp the powers of fable
By wits alone;
If wits could flick up fire
As smooth as breath to nostril,
Your ribs would glow,
Your chest become a brazier—
Of all mankind
The final opportunist!

Truth

Some can leave the truth unspoken.
Oh truth is light on such!
They may choose their time and season,
Nor feel it matters much.

I am not their judge, God help me!
Though I am of the crew
For whom is only truth or treason—
No choice between the two.

But pity wrestles with my fury
Till, spent and dumb and dry,
I envy bees which, barbed with reason,
Give the whole sting and die.

Victory

It comes to this, in plain words,
You will be defeated
By those who have no arms
And have not even retreated.

Back to original night
You will drive each defenceless city,
But in the eyes underground
There will be only pity.

Though, in contempt of life,
You slew the last defying,
Into your very ranks
His spirit would come flying.

When the learned have all despaired
For liberty departed,

31

This planet will be saved
By the simple-hearted.

More even, the universe,
Since space and time are shrinking!
What our star takes to heart
Its kind may yet be thinking.

The gentle are used to destroy
But the ultimate peace shall hinge
By an awful equity
On their unsought revenge.

It may even be
That under their frozen woe,
Bearing and bearing down,
You will snap like boughs in snow.

The humble shall sentence in kind
Those who winter the world by law,
Some may not be slain but live,
Forgotten in the thaw.

A. R. D. FAIRBURN

Rhyme of the Dead Self

Tonight I have taken all that I was
and strangled him that pale lily-white lad
I have choked him with these my hands these claws
catching him as he lay a-dreaming in his bed.

Then chuckling I dragged out his foolish brains
that were full of pretty love-tales heigho the holly
and emptied them holus bolus to the drains
those dreams of love oh what ruinous folly.

He is dead pale youth and he shall not rise
on the third day or any other day
sloughed like a snakeskin there he lies
and he shall not trouble me again for aye.

Winter Night

The candles gutter and burn out,
    and warm and snug we take our ease,
and faintly comes the wind's great shout
    as he assails the frozen trees.

The vague walls of this little room
    contract and close upon the soul;
deep silence hangs amid the gloom;
    no sound but the small voice of the coal.

Here in this sheltered firelit place
    we know not wind nor shivering tree;
we two alone inhabit space,
    locked in our small infinity.

This is our world, where love enfolds
   all images of joy, all strife
resolves in peace: this moment holds
   within its span the sum of life.

For Time's a ghost: these reddening coals
   were forest once ere he'd begun,
and now from dark and timeless boles
   we take the harvest of the sun;

and still the flower-lit solitudes
   are radiant with the springs he stole
where violets in those buried woods
   wake little blue flames in the coal.

Great stars may shine above this thatch;
   beyond these walls perchance are men
with laws and dreams: but our thin latch
   holds all such things beyond our ken.

The fire now lights our cloudy walls,
   now fails beneath the singing pot,
and as the last flame leaps and falls
   the far wall is and then is not.

Now lovelier than firelight is the gleam
   of dying embers, and your face
shines through the pathways of my dream
   like young leaves in a forest place.

from *Dominion*

Utopia

III

In the suburbs the spirit of man
walks on the garden path,
walks on the well-groomed lawn, dwells
among the manicured shrubs.
The variegated hedge encircles life.
In the countryside, in shire and county,
the abode of wind and sun, where clouds trample the sky
and hills are stretched like arms heaped up with bounty,
in the countryside the land is
the space between the barbed-wire fences,
mortgaged in bitterness, measured in sweated butterfat.

VI

The press: slow dripping of water on mud;
thought's daily bagwash, ironing out opinion,
scarifying the edges of ideas.
And the hirelings; caught young;
the bough bent and twisted
to the shape of evil; tending the oaf
who by accident of birth has property
in the public conscience, a 'moulder of opinion';
turning misshapen vessels, and jars for subtle poisons;
blinde mouthes;
insulated against discontent
born dumb and tractable, swift to disremember
the waif, and the hurt eyes of the passing stranger,
and the statistics of those who killed themselves
or were confined in asylums for the insane.

And the proletarian animal,
product of perversion and source of profit,
with a net paid circulation of a million,
and many unsold, or lying about the streets
bearing the marks of boot-protectors;
a crucified ape, preached by Darwinian bishops,
guarded by traitorous pens, handed the vinegar
of a 'belief in the essential goodness of human nature'.

IX

This is our paper city, built
on the rock of debt, held fast
against all winds by the paperweight of debt.
The crowds file slowly past, or stop and stare,
and here and there, dull-eyed, the idle stand
in clusters in the mouths of gramophone shops
in a blare of music that fills the crumpled air
with paper flowers and artificial scents
and painless passion in a heaven
of fancied love.
       The women come
from the bargain shops and basements
at dusk, as gazelles from drinking;
the men buy evening papers, scan them
for news of doomsday, light their pipes:
and the night sky, closing over, covers like a hand
the barbaric yawn of a young and wrinkled land.

from Album Leaves

Imperial

In the first days, in the forgotten calendars,
came the seeds of the race, the forerunners:
offshoots, outcasts, entrepreneurs,
architects of Empire, romantic adventurers;
and the famished, the multitude of the poor;
crossed parallels of boredom, tropics
of hope and fear, losing the pole-star, suffering
world of water, chaos of wind and sunlight,
and the formless image in the mind;
sailed under Capricorn to see for ever
the arc of the sun to northward.

They shouted at the floating leaf,
laughed with joy at the promise of life,
hope becoming belief, springing
alive, alight, gulls at the masthead crying,
the crag splitting the sky, slowly
towering out of the sea, taking
colour and shape, and the land
swelling beyond; noises
of water among rocks, voices singing.

Haven of hunger; landfall of hope;
goal of ambition, greed, and despair.

In tangled forests under the gloom
of leaves in the green twilight,
among the habitations of the older gods
they walked, with Christ beside them,
and an old enemy at hand, one whose creed
flourished in virgin earth. They divided the land;
some for their need, and some
for aimless, customary greed

that hardened with the years, grew taut
and knotted like a fist. Flower and weed
scattered upon the breeze
their indiscriminate seed; on every hillside fought
God's love against the old antagonist.
They change the sky but not their hearts who cross the seas.

These islands;
the remnant peaks of a lost continent,
roof of an old world, molten droppings
from earth's bowels, gone cold;
ribbed with rock, resisting the sea's corrosion
for an age, and an age to come. Of three races
the home: two passing in conquest
or sitting under the leaves, or on shady doorsteps
with quiet hands, in old age, childless.
And we, the latest: their blood on our hands: scions
of men who scaled ambition's
tottering slopes, whose desires
encompassed earth and heaven: we have prospered greatly,
we, the destined race, rulers of conquered isles,
sprouting like bulbs in warm darkness, putting out
white shoots under the wet sack of Empire.

Back Street

A girl comes out of a doorway in the morning
with hair uncombed, treading with care
on the damp bricks, picks up the milk,
stares skyward with sleepy eyes;
returns to the dewy step; leaves
with the closing of the door
silence under narrow eaves
the tragic scent of violets on the morning air
and jonquils thrust through bare earth here and there.

At ten o'clock a woman comes out
and leans against the wall
beside the fig-tree hung with washing; listens
for the postman's whistle. Soon he passes,
leaves no letter.
She turns a shirt upon the barren tree
and pads back to the house as ghost to tomb.
No children since the first. The room
papered in 'Stars', with Jubilee pictures
pasted over the mantel, spattered with fat.

Up the street
the taxi-drivers lounging in a knot
beside the rank of shining cars
discuss the speed of horses
as mariners the stars in their courses.

Conversation in the Bush

'Observe the young and tender frond
of this punga: shaped and curved
like the scroll of a fiddle: fit instrument
to play archaic tunes.'
                                    'I see
the shape of a coiled spring.'

Elements

I

In the summer we rode in the clay country,
the road before us trembling in the heat
and on the warm wind the scent of tea-tree,
grey and wind-bitten in winter, odorous under summer noon,
with spurts of dust under the hoofs
and a crackle of gorse on the wayside farms.
At dusk the sun fell down in violet hills
and evening came and we turned our horses
homeward through dewy air.

In autumn, kindness of earth, covering life,
mirrored stillness,
peace of mind, and time to think;
good fishing, and burdened orchards. Winter come,
headlands loomed in mist,
hills were hailswept, flowers were few;
and when we rode on the mountains in frosty weather
the distant ranges ran like blue veins through the land.
In spring we thrust our way through the bush,
through the ferns in the deep shadow angled with sunbeams,
roamed by streams in the bush, by the scarred stones
and the smooth stones water-worn, our shoulders wet
with rain from the shaken leaves.

O lovely time! when bliss was taken
as the bird takes nectar from the flower.
Happy the sunlit hour, the frost and the heat.
Hearts poised at a star's height
moved in a cloudless world
like gulls afloat above islands.

Smoke out of Europe, death blown
on the wind, and a cloak of darkness for the spirit.

II

Land of mountains and running water
rocks and flowers
and the leafy evergreen, O natal earth,
the atoms of your children
are bonded to you for ever:
though the images of your beauty lie in shadow,
time nor treachery, nor the regnant evil,
shall efface from the hearts of your children
from their eyes and from their fingertips
the remembrance of good.

Treading your hills, drinking your waters,
touching your greenness, they are content, finding
peace at the heart of strife
and a core of stillness in the whirlwind.
Absent, estranged from you, they are unhappy,
crying for you continually
in the night of their exile.

III

To prosper in a strange land
taking cocktails at twilight behind the hotel curtains,
buying cheap and selling dear, acquiring customs,
is to bob up and down like a fisherman's gaudy float
in a swift river.

He who comes back returns
to no ruin of gold nor riot of buds,
moan of doves in falling woods
nor wind of spring shaking the hedgerows,
heartsache, strangling sweetness: pictures
of change, extremes of time and growth,
making razor-sharp the tenses,
waking remembrance, torturing sense;

home-coming, returns only
to the dull green, hider of bones,
changeless, save in the slight spring
when the bush is peopled with flowers,
sparse clusters of white and yellow
on the dull green, like laughter in court;
and in summer when the coasts
bear crimson bloom, sprinkled like blood
on the lintel of the land.

Fairest earth,
fount of life, giver of bodies,
deep well of our delight, breath of desire,
let us come to you
barefoot, as befits love,
as the boy to the trembling girl,
as the child to the mother:
seeking before all things the honesty of substance,
touch of soil and wind and rock,
frost and flower and water,
the honey of the senses, the food
of love's imagining; and the most intimate
touch of love, that turns to being;
deriving wisdom, and the knowledge of necessity;
building thereon, stone by stone,
the rational architecture of truth, to house
the holy flame, that is neither reason nor unreason
but the thing given,
the flame that burns blue in the stillness, hovering
between the green wood of the flesh and the smoke of death.

Fair earth, we have broken our idols:
and after the days of fire we shall come to you
for the stones of a new temple.

Full Fathom Five

He was such a curious lover of shells
and the hallucinations of water
that he could never return out of the sea
without first having to settle a mermaid's bill.

Groping along the sea-bottom of the age
he discovered many particulars he did not care to speak about
even in the company of water-diviners
things sad and unspeakable
moss-covered skulls with bodies fluttering inside
with the unreality of specks moving before the eyes of a
        photograph
trumpets tossed from the decks of ocean-going liners
eccentric starfish fallen from impossible heavens
fretting on uncharted rocks
still continents with trees and houses like a child's drawing
and in every cupboard of the ocean
weary dolphins trapped in honey-coloured cobwebs
murmuring to the revolution Will you be long.

He was happy down there under the frothing ship-lanes
because nobody ever bothered him with statistics
or talk of yet another dimension of the mind.

And eventually and tragically finding he could not drown
he submitted himself to the judgement of the desert
and was devoured by man-eating ants
with a rainbow of silence branching from his lips.

Tapu

To stave off disaster, or bring the devil to heel,
    or to fight against fear, some carry a ring or a locket,
but I, who have nothing to lose by the turn of the wheel,
    and nothing to gain, I carry the world in my pocket.

For all I have gained, and have lost, is locked up in this
        thing,
    this cup of cracked bone from the skull of a fellow long
        dead,
with a hank of thin yellowish hair fastened in with a ring.
    For a symbol of death and desire these tokens are wed.

43

The one I picked out of a cave in a windy cliff-face
    where the old Maoris slept, with a curse on the stranger
        who moved,
  in despite of tapu, but a splinter of bone from that place.
  The other I cut from the head of the woman I loved.

Epithalamium

We have found our peace, and move with a turning globe;
the night is all about us, the lovers' robe.

Mortal my love, my strength: your beauty their wound.
Strip quickly darling, your fingers be the wind

undressing a snowy peak to the sun's love,
scatter your clouds, be Everest, O my Eve.

Leap on the bed, lie still, your body truth become dream
torturing my arms before their kingdom come.

Give the wise their negations, the moralists their maps;
our empire the moment, the geometer's point where all shapes

of delight are hidden as joy sleeps in the vine.
I tell you again, what the poor have always known,

that this is all the heaven we shall ever find
in all our footsore and fatal journey and beyond,

and we shall never have enough to keep out foul weather,
or to eke out age, will perish forgetful of each other,

yet breeding saints or subduing Asia set against this
were violating our lives with littleness.

Now at the brink of being, in our pride of blood
let us remember lost lovers, think of the dead

who have no power, who aching in earth lie,
the million bones, white longings in the night of eternity.

O love, how many of our faith have fallen!
Endless the torrent of time, endless and swollen

with tributaries from the broken veins of lovers.
I kiss you in remembrance of all true believers.

Midnight thoughts. Dark garlands to adorn your flesh
so it shine like snow, like fire. Flakes of ash

blowing from doom's far hill. Such wisps of terror
gazed at too long even in your body's mirror

would disrupt our continent, drain our seas,
bring all to nothing. Love, let us laugh and kiss,

only your lips but not with speech can tell
moving in the darkness what is unspeakable,

and though your eyes reflect spring's green and yellow like a pool
I cannot see them, can only guess at what is more beautiful

than home at last, than a child's sleep, more full of pity
and gentleness than snow falling on a burning city.

The Cave

From the cliff-top it appeared a place of defeat,
the nest of an extinct bird, or the hole where the sea hoards
   its bones,
a pocket of night in the sun-faced rock,
sole emblem of mystery and death in that enormous noon.

We climbed down, and crossed over the sand,
and there were islands floating in the wind-whipped blue,
and clouds and islands trembling in your eyes,
and every footstep and every glance
was a fatality felt and unspoken, our way
rigid and glorious as the sun's path,
unbroken as the genealogy of man.

And when we had passed beyond
into the secret place and were clasped
by the titanic shadows of the earth,
all was transfigured, all was redeemed,
so that we escaped from the days
that had hunted us like wolves, and from ourselves,
in the brief eternity of the flesh.

There should be the shapes of leaves and flowers
printed on the rock, and a blackening of the walls
from the flame on your mouth,
to be found by the lovers straying
from the picnic two worlds hence, to be found and known,
because the form of the dream is always the same,
and whatever dies or changes this will persist and recur,
will compel the means and the end, find consummation,
whether it be
silent in swansdown and darkness, or in grass moonshadow-
   mottled,
or in a murmuring cave of the sea.

We left, and returned to our lives:

the act entombed, its essence caught
for ever in the wind, and in the noise of waves,
for ever mixed
with lovers' breaths who by salt-water coasts
in the sea's beauty dwell.

A Farewell

What is there left to be said?
There is nothing we can say,
nothing at all to be done
to undo the time of day;
no words to make the sun
roll east, or raise the dead.

I loved you as I love life:
the hand I stretched out to you
returning like Noah's dove
brought a new earth to view,
till I was quick with love;
but Time sharpens his knife,

Time smiles and whets his knife,
and something has got to come out
quickly, and be buried deep,
not spoken or thought about
or remembered even in sleep.
You must live, get on with your life.

For an Amulet

What truly is will have no end,
although denied by friend or foe,
and this I tell to foe and friend
as onward to the grave we go.

The candle in my little room
gives light but will not bake the host.
I share my certainty with Hume,
my candle with the Holy Ghost.

The Estuary

The wind has died, no motion now
in the summer's sleepy breath. Silver the sea-grass,
the shells and the driftwood, fixed in the moon's vast
    crystal.
Think: long after, when the walls of the small house
have collapsed upon us, each alone,
far gone the earth's invasion
the slow earth bedding and filling the bone,
this water will still be crawling up the estuary,
fingering its way among the channels, licking the stones;
and the floating shells, minute argosies
under the giant moon, still shoreward glide
among the mangroves on the creeping tide.

The noise of gulls comes through the shining darkness
over the dunes and the sea. Now the clouded moon
is warm in her nest of light. The world's a shell
where distant waves are murmuring of a time
beyond this time. *Give me the ghost of your hand:*
unreal, unreal the dunes,
the sea, the mangroves, and the moon's white light,
unreal, beneath our naked feet, the sand.

Solitude

The curtains in the solemn room
    are drawn against the winter dusk;
the lady sitting in the gloom
    has hair that faintly smells of musk.

As in some dim romantic night
    the mist will not divulge the moon,
around her unbetrothèd plight
    her thoughts have woven a cocoon.

Now recollection brings again
    the distant hour, the tide that flowed,
the word that might have flowered then
    as epic or as episode.

Half proud because the thing she sought,
    still lacking, is inviolate,
half puzzled by that eerie thought
    she rocks her chair and scans the grate.

Then suddenly she sees it clear,
    the monstrous image, cold, precise—
the body of the mountaineer
    preserved within the glacial ice,
      for ever safe, where none shall seek,
      beneath the unattempted peak.

I'm Older than You,
Please Listen

To the young man I would say:
Get out! Look sharp, my boy,
before the roots are down,
before the equations are struck,
before a face or a landscape
has power to shape or destroy.
This land is a lump without leaven,
a body that has no nerves.
Don't be content to live in
a sort of second-grade heaven
with first-grade butter, fresh air,
and paper in every toilet;
becoming a butt for the malice
of those who have stayed and soured,
staying in turn to sour,
to smile, and savage the young.
If you're enterprising and able,
smuggle your talents away,
hawk them in livelier markets
where people are willing to pay.
If you have no stomach for roughage,
if patience isn't your religion,
if you must have sherry with your bitters,
if money and fame are your pigeon,
if you feel that you need success
and long for a good address,
don't anchor here in the desert—
the fishing isn't so good:
take a ticket for Megalopolis,
don't stay in this neighbourhood!

Down on My Luck

Wandering above a sea of glass
   in the soft April weather,
wandering through the yellow grass
   where the sheep stand and blether;
roaming the cliffs in the morning light,
   hearing the gulls that cry there,
not knowing where I'll sleep tonight,
   not much caring either.

    I haven't got a stiver
      the tractor's pinched my job,
    I owe the bar a fiver
      and the barman fifteen bob;
    the good times are over,
      the monkey-man has foreclosed,
    the woman has gone with the drover,
      not being what I supposed.

    I used to set things spinning,
      I used to dress like a lord,
    mostly I came out winning,
      but all that's gone by the board;
    my pants have lost their creases,
      I've fallen down on my luck,
    the world has dropped to pieces,
      everything's come unstuck.

Roaming the cliffs in the morning light,
   hearing the gulls that cry there,
not knowing where I'll sleep tonight,
   not much caring either,
wandering above a sea of glass
   in the soft April weather,
wandering through the yellow grass
   close to the end of my tether.

R. A. K. MASON

Old Memories of Earth

I think I have no other home than this
    I have forgotten much remember much
    but I have never any memories such
    as these make out they have of lands of bliss.

Perhaps they have done, will again do what
    they say they have, drunk as gods on godly drink,
    but I have not communed with gods I think
    and even though I live past death shall not.

I rather am for ever bondaged fast
    to earth and have been: so much untaught I know.
    Slow like great ships often I have seen go
    ten priests ten each time round a grave long past

And I recall I think I can recall
    back even past the time I started school
    or went a-crusoeing in the corner pool
    that I was present at a city's fall

And I am positive that yesterday
    walking past One Tree Hill and quite alone
    to me there came a fellow I have known
    in some old times, but when I cannot say:

Though we must have been great friends, I and he,
    otherwise I should not remember him
    for everything of the old life seems dim
    as last year's deeds recalled by friends to me.

Body of John

Oh I have grown so shrivelled and sere
    But the body of John enlarges
    and I can scarcely summon a tear
    but the body of John discharges

It's true my old roof is near ready to drop
    But John's boards have burst asunder
    and I am perishing cold here atop
    but his bones lie stark hereunder.

Sonnet of Brotherhood

Garrisons pent up in a little fort
    with foes who do but wait on every side
    knowing the time soon comes when they shall ride
    triumphant over those trapped and make sport
    of them: when those within know very short
    is now their hour and no aid can betide:
    such men as these not quarrel and divide
    but friend and foe are friends in their hard sort

And if these things be so oh men then what
    of these beleaguered victims this our race
    betrayed alike by Fate's gigantic plot
    here in this far-pitched perilous hostile place
    this solitary hard-assaulted spot
    fixed at the friendless outer edge of space.

The Spark's Farewell to Its Clay

I

Well clay it's strange at last we've come to it:
 after much merriment we must give up
 our ancient friendship: no more shall we sup
 in pleasant quiet places wanly-lit
 nor wander through the falling rain, sharp-smit
 and buffeted you, while I within snug-shut:
 no longer taste the mingled bitter-sweet cup
 of life the one inscrutable has thought fit

To give to us: no longer know the strife
 that we from old have each with each maintained:
 now our companionship has certain end
 end without end: at last of this our life
 you surely have gained blank earth walls
     my friend
 and I? God only knows what I have gained.

II

There is no thought that any hope can give
 for this fine hair and these long pliant hands
 and this proud body that so firmly stands
 these eyes deep delicate and sensitive:
 vain vain for such in mind towards hope to strive.
 What if my body has at its commands
 strength beauty knowledge rule of many lands
 still is not any hope that it can live.

Perhaps I seek myself and am not whole:
 times think I in some pure place there can wait
 a far surpassing fellow for my soul
 and joy to think when I shall find that mate—
 still you good easy earth must pay earth-toll
 I recollect and so am desolate.

54

Latter-day Geography Lesson

This, quoth the Eskimo master
    was London in English times:
    step out a little bit faster
    you two young men at the last there
    the Bridge would be on our right hand
    and the Tower near where those crows stand—
    we struck it you'll recall in Gray's rhymes:
    this, quoth the Eskimo master
    was London in English times.

This, quoth the Eskimo master
    was London in English days:
    beyond that hill they called Clapham
    boys that swear Master Redtooth I slap 'em
    I dis-tinct-ly heard—you—say—Bastard
    don't argue: here boys, ere disaster
    overtook her, in splendour there lay
    a city held empires in sway
    and filled all the earth with her praise:
    this, quoth the Eskimo master
    was London in English days.

She held, quoth the Eskimo master
    ten million when her prime was full
    from here once Britannia cast her
    gaze over an Empire vaster
    even than ours: look there Woking
    stood, I make out, and the Abbey
    lies here under our feet *you great babby*
    Swift-and-short do—please—kindly—stop—poking
    your thumbs through the eyes of that skull.

Song of Allegiance

Shakespeare Milton Keats are dead
  Donne lies in a lowly bed

Shelley at last calm doth lie
  knowing 'whence we are and why'

Byron Wordsworth both are gone
  Coleridge Beddoes Tennyson

Housman neither knows nor cares
  how 'this heavy world' now fares

Little clinging grains enfold
  all the mighty minds of old . . .

They are gone and I am here
  stoutly bringing up the rear

Where they went with limber ease
  toil I on with bloody knees

Though my voice is cracked and harsh
  stoutly in the rear I march

Though my song have none to hear
  boldly bring I up the rear.

Oils and Ointments

Let me fall down about your feet oh Christ
  that have bruised and bled along the lonely way,
wait here my bringing forth those highly priced
treasures I have saved up this many a day.

The ointments I bring up to you my lord
  gleam jewels like a steel-flashing beetle shard
  lo! I shower down cascading the rich hoard
  frankincense aloes myrrh cassia spikenard,

Sluggish oil that glints oh look rainbows and gold
  gently assailing unguents the orient has spiced
  slow pouring balm smooth smearing calm behold
  and stretch out your soothful longing foot oh Christ.

Nails and a Cross

Nails and a cross and crown of thorn,
  here I die the mystery-born:
  here's an end to adventurings
  here all great and valiant things
  find as far as I'm concerned a grave.

God, I may say that I've been brave
  and it's led me——? Damned and deified
  here I spurt the blood from a riven side:
  blood, never revisit my heart again
  but suck the wisdom out of my brain
  I got in so many lonely days
  bruising my feet with flinty ways.

For I left my boyhood dog and fire
  my old bed and him I called my sire
  my mother my village my books and all
  to follow the wild and lonely call
  luring me into the solitary
  road that has brought me here to die.

And I see, if I squint, my blood of death
　　drip on the little harsh grass beneath
　　and friend and foe and men long dead
　　faint and reel in my whirling head:
　　and while the troops divide up my cloak
　　the mob fling dung and see the joke.

If the Drink

If the drink that satisfied
　　the son of Mary when he died
　　has not the right smack for you
　　leave it for a kindlier brew.

For my bitter verses are
　　sponges steeped in vinegar
　　useless to the happy-eyed
　　but handy for the crucified.

On the Swag

His body doubled
　　under the pack
　　that sprawls untidily
　　on his old back
　　the cold wet dead-beat
　　plods up the track.

The cook peers out:
　　'oh curse that old lag—
　　here again
　　with his clumsy swag
　　made of a dirty old
　　turnip bag.'

'Bring him in cook
    from the grey level sleet
    put silk on his body
    slippers on his feet,
    give him fire
    and bread and meat.

Let the fruit be plucked
    and the cake be iced,
    the bed be snug
    and the wine be spiced
    in the old cove's night-cap:
    for this is Christ.'

Judas Iscariot

Judas Iscariot
    sat in the upper
    room with the others
    at the last supper

And sitting there smiled
    up at his master
    whom he knew the morrow
    would roll in disaster.

At Christ's look he guffawed—
    for then as thereafter
    Judas was greatly
    given to laughter,

Indeed they always said
    that he was the veriest
    prince of good fellows
    and the whitest and merriest.

All the days of his life
he lived gay as a cricket
and would sing like the thrush
that sings in the thicket

He would sing like the thrush
that sings on the thorn
oh he was the most sporting bird
that ever was born.

Footnote to John ii. 4

Don't throw your arms around me in that way:
I know that what you tell me is the truth—
yes I suppose I loved you in my youth
as boys do love their mothers, so they say,
but all that's gone from me this many a day:
I am a merciless cactus an uncouth
wild goat a jagged old spear the grim tooth
of a lone crag . . . Woman I cannot stay.

Each one of us must do his work of doom
and I shall do it even in despite
of her who brought me in pain from her womb,
whose blood made me, who used to bring the light
and sit on the bed up in my little room
and tell me stories and tuck me up at night.

Ecce Homunculus

Betrayed by friend dragged from the garden hailed
as prophet and as lord in mockery
hauled down where Roman Pilate sat on high
perplexed and querulous, lustily assailed

by every righteous Hebrew cried down railed
against by all true zealots—still no sigh
escaped him but he boldly went to die
made scarcely a moan when his soft flesh was nailed.

And so he brazened it out right to the last
still wore the gallant mask still cried 'Divine
am I, lo for me is heaven overcast'
though that inscrutable darkness gave no sign
indifferent or malignant: while he was passed
by even the worst of men at least sour wine.

The Young Man Thinks of Sons

Did my father curse his father for his lust I wonder
            as I do mine
and my grand-dad curse his sire for his wickedness his weakness
  his blunder
            and so on down the whole line

Well I'll stop the game break the thread end my race: I will not
  continue
            in the old bad trade:
I'll take care that for my nerveless mind weakened brain neglected
  sinew
            I alone shall have paid.

Let the evil book waste in its swathings the ill pen write not one
  iota
            the ship of doom not sail,
let the sword rot unused in its scabbard let the womb lack its
  quota:
            here let my line fail:

Let the plough rust untouched of the furrow, yea let the blind
semen
                    stretch vain arms for the virgin:
I'll hammer no stringed harps for gods to clash discords, or
women:
                    my orchard won't burgeon.

I'll take care that the lust of my loins never bring to fruition
                    the seed of a son
who in his nettle-grown kingdom should curse both my sins of
commission
                    and what I left undone.

Lugete O Veneres

With his penis swollen for the girl on the next farm and rigid
                    here he lies on his bed
motionless dumb and his naked corpse goose-fleshed and as frigid
                    as if he were dead:

Only at times a great sob rises up in his drawn aching throttle
                    and dies like his hope
or the tear of his anguish drips down on his arm cold and mottled
                    like a bar of blue soap.

For the people next door have packed up their pots and their
table
                    and their mats and their ploughs
they have brought up their pigs from the sty their steeds from
the stable
                    and driven off the cows.

62

Tomorrow strange people will reign there tomorrow the stranger
               will inherit their places
other cows know the shed where they milk, new horses the
    manger
               and dogs with unknown faces.

Mark how dejected tormented he lies poor lad while shivers
               run and shake his fat arse:
for a space let us mourn here this tortured boy's slobbering
    quivers
               as we laugh at the farce.

Our Love was a Grim Citadel

Our love was a grim citadel:
    no tawdry plaything for the minute
    of strong dark stone we built it well
    and based in the ever-living granite:

The urgent columns of the years
    press on, like tall rain up the valley:
    and Chaos bids ten thousand spears
    run to erase our straw-built folly.

Flow at Full Moon

Your spirit flows out over all the land between
    your spirit flows out as gentle and limpid as milk
    flows on down ridge and through valley as soft and serene
    as the light of the moon that sifts down through its light
               sieve of silk

63

The long fingers of the flow press forward, the whole hand follows
    easily the fingers creep they're your hair's strands that curl
    along the land's brow, your hair dark-bright gleaming on
        heights and hollows
    and the moon illumines the flow with mother of pearl

Beloved your love is poured to enchant all the land
    the great bull falls still the opossum turns from his chatter
    and the thin nervous cats pause and the strong oak-trees
        stand
    entranced and the gum's restless bark-strip is stilled from its
        clatter

Your spirit flows out from your deep and radiant nipples
    and the whole earth turns tributary all her exhalations
    wave up in white breath and are absorbed in the ripples
    that pulse like a bell along the blood from your body's
        pulsations

And as the flow settles down to the sea it nets me about
    with a noose of one soft arm stretched out from its course:
    oh loved one my dreams turn from sleep: I shall rise and
        go out
    and float my body into the flow and press back till I find
        its source.

ROBIN HYDE

The Bronze Rider, Wellington

Riding wooden horses from the hot Christmas Caves,
The children came laughing out into the Quay,
With a prance at their hills, and a dash at their waves,
And the broad street between shining peaceful and free.
Cheeks nipped in the wind, and their curls sailing gold,
Rode the sons and the daughters . . . (Come home, dears,
       come home.)
But a wind from the sea blows, a thin mist blows cold . . .
Faint down the Quay sounds the tuck of a drum.

Children, come home, and be kissed as you're told.
(Ah, but who said it? A child could grow old.)
Home when you're bid, or the length of my tongue.
(Ah, but who said it? A child could die young.)
Now the bronze Rider comes to stay awhile,
In our hilly heart, so haunted by running feet;
Turns to the dusk his young, mysterious smile,
Implacably, unanswerably sweet.
He props the sky up with his stiff young arm,
Lest down it drop on cradled cottages,
Do our poor groping ways of living harm,
Vex with a light our city, that was his.
O forfeit of this world. . . . The great bronze hooves,
Soundless, yet trampling air as they aspire,
Fling shame on us, who tread the ancient grooves;
Dawn is his stirrup, and his reins are fire.

Riding painted horses from town to Island Bay,
Mouths pink as moss-roses, hair sailing free,
Past the penny-shops, awning-shops, red shops and grey,
Past the vast jars of peppermint down to the sea;
Past the Blue Platter Inn, that's been burnt seven year,

Ride the sons and the daughters. (Come home, loves,
        come home.)
But the sound of a bugle folds crisp on the air,
The swish of a keel cutting out in the foam.

Children, come home, will you hear your Dad shout?
(Ah, but who said it? A ship could glide out . . .)
Home to your broth and your books, as you're bid . . .
(Ah, but who cried it? Our lamps could be hid.)

Faint on the Quay sounds the throb of the drum.

The Last Ones

But the last black horse of all
Stood munching the green-bud wind,
And the last of the raupo huts
Let down its light behind.
Sullen and shadow-clipped
He tugged at the evening star,
New-mown silvers swished like straw
Across the manuka.

As for the hut, it said
No word but its meagre light,
Its people slept as the dead,
Bedded in Maori night.
'And there is the world's last door,
And the last world's horse,' sang the wind,
'With little enough before,
And what you have seen behind.'

from *The Beaches*

VI

Close under here, I watched two lovers once,
Which should have been a sin, from what you say:
I'd come to look for prawns, small pale-green ghosts,
Sea-coloured bodies tickling round the pool.
But tide was out then; so I strolled away
And climbed the dunes, to lie here warm, face down,
Watching the swimmers by the jetty-posts
And wrinkling like the bright blue wrinkling bay.
It wasn't long before they came; a fool
Could see they had to kiss; but your pet dunce
Didn't quite know men count on more than that;
And so just lay, patterning the sand.
                And they
Were pale thin people, not often clear of town;
Elastic snapped, when he jerked off her hat;
I heard her arguing, 'Dick, my frock!' But he
Thought she was bread.
I wished her legs were brown,
And mostly, then, stared at the dawdling sea,
Hoping Perry would row me some day in his boat.

Not all the time; and when they'd gone, I went
Down to the hollow place where they had been,
Trickling bed through fingers. But I never meant
To tell the rest, or you, what I had seen;
Though that night, when I came in late for tea,
I hoped you'd see the sandgrains on my coat.

from *The Houses*

I

Old nursery chair; its legs, cut down, are broken:
Old timepiece, out-of-date, forlorn and slow:
Slow creaking shadow; somebody unawoken.
Trumpet: don't touch it, soldier, it won't blow.

III

Adolicus; that's a creeper rug, its small
Pink-and-white piecemeal flowers swarm down a fence:
So little, no scent to be by; show, pretence—
Nothing to do, but hide the rotting wall.
Three slats were broken: but the street-boys' eyes
Can't climb in here like ants and frighten us.
Stare if they like: we've the adolicus.

V

None of it true; for Christ's sake, spill the ink,
Tear out this charnel's darnel-root, that lingers
Sprouting words, words, words! Give me cool bluegum
       leaves
To rub brittle between my fingers.

I had the touch of hillside once: the ever-
So-slender cold of buttercup stems in brink:
Pebbles: great prints in mud: Oh, Lazarus, bring me
Some mountain honesty to drink!

Pihsien Road

Old men in blue: and heavily encumbered
Old shoulders held by shadowy whips in sway,
Like ox and ass, that down this road have lumbered
All day: all the bright murderous day.
More than their stumbling footprints press this clay.

And light in air, pure white, in wonder riding,
Some crazy Phaeton these have never known
Holds by a lever their last awe, deciding
How flesh shall spurt from sinews, brain from bone—
Crushing desolate grain with a harder stone.

What Is It Makes the Stranger?

What is it makes the stranger? Say, oh eyes!
Because I was journeying far, sailing alone,
Changing one belt of stars for the northern belt,
Men in my country told me, 'You will be strange—
Their ways are not our ways; not like ourselves
They think, suffer, and dream.'
So sat I silent, and watched the stranger, why he was strange.
But now, having come so far, shed the eight cloaks of wind,
Ridden ponies of foam, and the great stone lions of six strange
cities.
What is it makes the stranger? Say, oh eyes!
Eyes cannot tell. They view the self-same world—
Outer eyes vacant till thoughts and pictures fill them,
Inner eyes watching secret paths of the brain.
Hands? But the hands of my country knit reeds, bend wood,
Shape the pliable parts of boats and roofs.
Mend pots, paint pictures, write books
Though different books; glean harvests, if different harvests,
Not so green as young rice first shaking its spears from water.

Hands cannot say. Feet then? They say
In shoe, not sandal, or bare if a man be poor,
They thread long ways between daylight and dark,
Longer, from birth to death.
Know flint from grasses, wear soles through, hate sharp pebbles,
Oftentimes long for the lightness of birds.
Yet in my country, children, even the poor
Wear soft warm shoes, and a little foot in the dance
Warms the looks of young men, no less than here.
In my country, on summer evenings, clean as milk poured out
From old blue basins, children under the hawthorne trees
Fly kites, lacing thin strings against the sky.
Not at New Year, but at other festivals
We light up fire-crackers
In memory of old buried danger, now a ghost danger.

On a roof garden, among the red-twigged bowing of winter
                    trees,
The small grave bowls of dwarf pines (our pines grow tall
Yet the needle-sharp hair is the same) one first star swam,
Silver in lily-root dusk. Two lovers looked up.
Hands, body, heart in my breast,
Whispered, 'These are the same. Here we are not so strange—
Here there are friends and peace.
We have known such ways, we in our country!'

Black-tiled roofs, curled like wide horns, and hiding safe
From the eyes of the stranger, all that puts faith in you.
Remember this, of an unknown woman who passed,
But who stood first high on the darkening roof garden looking
                    down.
My way behind me tattered away in wind,
Before me, was spelt with strange letters.
My mind was a gourd heavy with sweet and bitter waters.
Since I could not be that young girl, who heedless of stars
Now watched the face of her lover,

I wished to be, for one day, a man selling mandarins,
A blackened tile in some hearth place; a brazier, a well, a good
	word,
A blackened corpse along the road to Chapei,
Of a brave man, dead for his country.
Shaking the sweet-bitter waters within my mind,
It seemed to me, all seas fuse and intermarry.
Under the seas, all lands knit fibre, interlock:
On a highway so ancient as China's
What are a few miles more to the ends of the earth?
Is another lantern too heavy to light up, showing the face
Of farers and wayfarers, stumbling the while they go,
Since the world has called them stranger?

Only two rebels cried out 'We do not understand.'
Ear said, 'China and we
Struck two far sides of a rock; music came forth,
Our music and theirs, not the one music.
Listening in street and stall I hear two words,
Their word and mine. Mine is not understood,
Therefore am I an exile here, a stranger,
Eaten up with hunger for what I understand,
And for that which understands.'
Tongue said, 'I know
The sweet flavours of mandarin or fish. But mouth and I,
Speaking here, are mocked. Looks fall on us like blows.
Mistress, we served you well, and not for cash,
But free men. Therefore, beseech you, let us go on.'

Heart, lowlier, said, 'There is a way of patience—
Let ear study the door to understanding.
Mouth, there is silence first, but fellowship
Where children laugh or weep, the grown smile or frown,
Study, perceive, and learn. Let not two parts
Unwisely make an exile of the whole.'

71

But still the rebels bawled, and so I saw
How in a world divorced from silences
These are the thieves.
Ear, who no longer listening well, sniffs up
The first vain trash, the first argument into his sack.
Mouth, who will spew it forth, but to be heard—
Both ill-taught scholars, credulous liars,
Seizing on, flinging up fuel.
There flamed the restlessness of such sick worlds,
As cannot know their country or earth's country;
Their moment or an age's moment.
Having such brawling servants in my train
I can be neither tile nor lamp.
Only a footprint. Some boy sees it at dawn
Before his high-wheeled cart creaks over it;
Only a sped and broken arrow,
Pointing a way where men will come in peace.

The Deserted Village

In the deserted village, sunken down
With a shrug of last weak old age, pulled back to earth,
All people are fled or killed. The cotton crop rots,
Not one mild house leans sideways, a man on crutches,
Not a sparrow earns from the naked floors,
Walls look, but cannot live without the folk they loved—
It would be a bad thing to awaken them.
Having broken the rice-bowl, seek not to fill it again.

The village temple, well built, with five smashed gods, ten
       whole ones,
Does not want prayers. It's last vain prayer bled up
When the women ran outside to be slain.
A temple must house its sparrows or fall asleep,
Therefore a long time, under his crown of snails,
The gilded Buddha demands to meditate.

72

No little flowering fires on the incense-strings
Startle Kwan-Yin, whom they dressed in satin—
Old women sewing beads like pearls in her hair.
This was a temple for the very poor ones:
Their gods were mud and lathe: but artfully
Some village painter coloured them all.
Wooden dragons were carefully carved.
Finding in mangled wood one smiling childish tree,
Roses and bells not one foot high,
I set it back, at the feet of Kwan-Yin.
A woman's prayer-bag,
Having within her paper prayers, paid for in copper,
Seeing it torn, I gathered it up.
I shall often think, 'The woman I did not see
Voiced here her dying wish.
But the gods dreamed on. So low her voice, so loud
The guns, all that death-night, who would stoop to hear?'

CHARLES BRASCH

The Islands (ii)

Always, in these islands, meeting and parting
Shake us, making tremulous the salt-rimmed air;
Divided, many-tongued, the sea is waiting,
Bird and fish visit us and come no more.
Remindingly beside the quays the white
Ships lie smoking; and from their haunted bay
The godwits vanish towards another summer.
Everywhere in light and calm the murmuring
Shadow of departure; distance looks our way;
And none knows where he will lie down at night.

Great Sea

Kona Coast, Hawaii

Speak for us, great sea.

Speak in the night, compelling
The frozen heart to hear,
The memoried to forget.
O speak, until your voice
Possess the night, and bless
The separate and fearful;
Under folded darkness
All the lost unite—
Each to each discovered,
Vowed and wrought by your voice
And in your life, that holds
And penetrates our life:
You from whom we rose,
In whom our power lives on.

74

All night, all night till dawn
Speak for us, great sea.

from *Nineteen Thirty-nine*

I

The City

The walls divide us from water and from light,
Fruits are sold but do not ripen here;
We cannot tell the time of year,
And lamps and traffic estrange us from the night.

What of our fellow-citizens, the doves
And sparrows that seem now to belong here? Could
They live as freely in hedgerow and in wood
After generations of town lives?

For we have shut ourselves off from the larger world
And grown hearts narrow like alleys; we are afraid
Of quiet, emptiness, the far away.

No one knows what his neighbour is called,
But fears him; defences go up; weapons are made
To keep the unknown constantly at bay.

III

Far on the mountains of pain there may yet be a place
For breath, where the insensate wind is still,
A hollow of stones where you can bow your face
And relax the quivering distended will.

There earth's life will speak to you again,
An insect in the grasses, a meagre bird,
That in that outpost faithfully maintain
The pulse of being so slowly, weakly heard.

And they remain. But you go on, and bear
The frail life farther yet, blindly and slow,
Into the pitiless mountains and the glare
Of deathly light, ceasing to know or care
If you are still man; but the frozen rocks know,
And the white wind massing against you as you go.

Photograph of a Baby

Round-head round-eyed Sebastian,
Wrinkling his eyes against the sun,
Looks into the distance and will not see anyone.

What does he find there
At the end of his absorbing stare,
Where Mt. Herbert floats weightless in the glass-clear air?

It is something he does not meet
Among us, that he will not be asked to greet,
To laugh at or yield to, because it knows how to treat

Him as an equal, as fact,
The present and plain, which neither bluffness nor tact
Can make more real or charm away or even distract.

Such he can understand,
It is primal like himself, like the sun on his hand,
Disdaining to raise a smoke-screen of reasons for what must
    be, and

76

Ignores all conditions. For though objects are multiplied
Hourly in his world, he cannot put them aside,
But always must try to see them as clearly as though they
    had died,

As still and as final; and he
Has the air of one looking back, by death set free,
Who sees the strangeness of life, and what things are trying
    to be.

Word by Night

Ask in one life no more
Than that first revelation of earth and sky,
Renewed as now in the place of birth
Where the sea turns and the first roots go down.

By the same light also you may know yourselves:
You are of those risen from the sea
And for ever bound to the sea,
Which is but the land's other and older face.

It is time to replant the seed of life
At this rich boundary where it first sprang,
For you are water and earth,
Creatures of the shore, disputed ground.

For too long now too many have been deceived,
Renouncing the bare nursery of the race,
Trying to shed the limiting names
That link them to their kind;

Have sought sufficiency
In the contingent and derivative,
Wishing to rise from doubtful earth
And move secure among the abstract stars;

But faltering, losing the prime sense of direction,
Fell at last in mindless lassitude
Among the traffic,
Chattering, withered, unrecognizable.

Come again to the shore, the gathering place,
Where cries of sea-birds wring the air,
And by the poverty of rocks remember
Human degrees.

Water rises through the sand, but near
Are the first pastures,
Dyed by the shadow of a leaf,
Promise of the mind's kingdoms.

Seasons that bore you bring renewal,
But do not alter
The nature of your never-finished nature,
Nor the condition of time.

Oreti Beach

Thunder of waves out of the dying west,
Thunder of time that overtakes our day;
Evening islands founder, gold sand turns grey
In ocean darkness where we walk possessed.

What does it mean, this clamorous fall of night
Upon the heart's stillness? What pledge can they give,
These passionate powers of the world, that we might live
More surely than by the soul's solitary light?

Letter from Thurlby Domain

I walk among my great-grandfather's trees.
Through poplar and pine pour the steady seas
Of mild mountain wind, norwester, in long-
Breathed tide and calm of voice shaking their strong
Rock-bedded roots; yet, below, the air is still
In this orchard-harbour deep embayed in the hill-
Terrace, where cattle graze in thick grass
By pear-tree, apricot, walnut, and through the ground-bass
Swell of the wind quivers and rings a thread
Of song from leaf-lost birds. But dumb and dead
In this quick summer stir the old house decays,
Hollow, unroofed, with staring window-bays
And boards torn up; from fallen foundations the stone
Walls lean outward; garrulous starlings own
It as home now, but after ninety years
No man any more.

            When a long-lived house disappears,
Ruined, into this raw-man's-land, and grows
New harvests of elder and thistle and briar rose,
An air of contentment breathes from it, almost
Of reconciliation, the laying of a ghost—
That figure of brute man breaking in on nature,
Defiling its sanctities, altering rhythm and feature,
That represents us all, that haunts all
Our works till they too are proved natural
By their decay, and so are lost to us
And given back to nature; like this house.

A debt is paid here then, a silent wrong
Atoned in silence, and one man's works belong
At last to earth. But man's earth: is it not now
Man's, marked with the sign of axe and plough,
Watered, shaded, settled? For men have brought
Ripe gifts to soften the rigours that contort

This towering snow-dazzled sun-shot world
Of rock on rock, mountain on mountain hurled,
Cupping cold lakes, bare valleys curved for sleep.

Look, he who built here planted: road, hedge, and sweep
Of fields, garden, and stable; this avenue
All summer sounding, cool in the blazing blue,
Its poplar-fountains soaring from some green well
Under the waste where there was nothing to tell
Of water's sweetness; and hill of twilight pine,
And the wind-censing gum's tattered ensign
Over the running grasses; ash, acacia,
Lime, and tall towers of wellingtonia—
All his; and he in Lebanon plucked the cone
From which that masterful cedar sprang alone;
He, my great-grandfather whom I did not know,
Who built and sowed and left his seed to grow
Cradling the land. So these rich groves (and those
That crown now the bare peninsula he chose
For Queenstown Park) make him a monument,
And marry us to this earth; but for the spent,
The sober house, that held so mildly together
Brunswick and Lincolnshire in colonial tether—
All trace of person gone, all family pride,
Call it man's first-fruits offered and not denied.

Cast on this Eden we must violate still,
Where shall we find that good for which we do ill
By necessity, but so long? Where, if not in
The heart's peace from which all worlds begin,
Our wrong and loss and pain with a due kiss
Sealed in acknowledgement of our genesis;
Not by inflaming nor by stilling desire,
But learning in the fire the nature of fire,
Upon the wheel replenishing the wheel,
Caught in the dance that sifts unreal from real.
Dead house and living trees and we that live

To make our peace on earth and become native
In place and time, in life and death: how should
We entertain any other goal or good
Than this, than here?
                              From Crown to Coronet
The sun has swung overhead, and burning yet
Thirsts for western waters; the wind will soon die
In the trees; at my foot a lizard slides among dry
Stalks and is gone with a flickering good-bye.

Autumn, Thurlby Domain

What news for man in a broken house, old trees
And ruined garden dying among the hills?
Nothing is here to distract or to surprise,
Nothing except the plainness of stone walls
And trunks unleafing, what has been planted and grows,
What has been built to stand; that now fails,
Having served its time,
And goes back ripe to the earth from which it came.

What news? Are old age and decay so new
They put us out of countenance, offend
Lives that have long forgotten how to grow
And die, and do not care to understand
The elemental language of sickle and plough,
Of nursery and orchard, sun and wind,
That speak to us everywhere
With the same untroubled intimacy as here?

What we have found before we shall find again,
No new thing; age and youth seem strange to us
Who can no longer relight the morning sun,
Bring each day to birth in that bitter stress

And eddying joy that mark the life of a man
As years ring a tree; only in loss,
All knowledge stripped away,
We stumble towards our naked identity.

All civilizations, all societies,
Die with a dying house. These walls beheld
Rites of birth, marriage and death, customary days
Of equable happiness, dear hope unfulfilled,
Heart practised in patience and hand grown wise;
All riddling glory men have dreamed or hailed
Lived here in embryo or
Epitome, and dies in character.

What ceremony does autumn hold this afternoon
With green-gold bough and golden spire—what rite
Of pirouetting poplar-dancers, to crown
The dying year, the death of man's estate,
With brilliance so raptly and so lightly worn?
In celebration of death we consummate
Our vows to place and time,
In sickness and in health to live and die with them.

Self to Self

'Out of this thoughtless, formless, swarming life
What can I find of form and thought to live by,
What can I take that will make my song news?'

'Where nothing is, a seed may yet be sown.
Does not chaos cry for the forming hand?
Thought and form be the new song you choose.'

'But if this outward chaos only mirrors
Chaos within, confusion at the heart,
How can I start, where settle to begin?'

'The formless and the thoughtless then your theme;
Knowing disorder like the palm of your hand,
Set up house there, amid the stench and din,

And be at home in your own darkness, naming
Hand and mouth first, wall and ceiling, then all
That hurts you or offends, without as within,

All that you hate, that maddens, that merely is—
The ants, the dumb oxen, the golden calves
(For there is nothing you have the right to refuse);

And when you have bent before them, made them one
With the waste heart, they will obey your word,
Out of disorder bring you song for news.'

'To work in what I fear, subject my weakness
To power, surrender speech for an idiot dumbness?—
O worse than death, the very self to abuse.'

'What have you left to lose, disorder's own?
Only from incarnation of disorder
Can order spring, and you must end to begin,
If you would sing you must become news.'

from *The Estate*

xxii

Once more as I gather about me the cloak of the evening,
Fastening windows, drawing curtains, and moving
Arm-chair, paper, and books to the lamp and the fireside
That now till morning shall be a world sufficient,
I turn to you calmly, after the day's distractions,

And picture you as I would, alert and thoughtful,
Almost unchanged since dawn, or only changed by
Putting on more completely the rounded nature
So seldom visible to me undistorted
Because I see it in many climates and under
Changing aspects, each with its partial purpose
(For though we divine the nature of those who are near to
    us
We do not see it entire, never exhaust it,
Not in a lifetime: to see another completely
Would mean to reveal oneself to him completely
—Or to see with a god's eye, stilled and unjudging—
And that is not in our power, not in the lover's
Nor in the mother's power, neither by willing
Nor yet by surrender); find you although familiar
Fresh, dewed with surprises, as if you bore the
Archaic smile of the morning-marvelling kouroi;
You take possession again of my city of silence;
You are the limitless dark defining the circle
Of fireside, lamplight; you the inconceivable
Guest out of nowhere suddenly fiery and singing
Before me, midnight word of transfiguration.

xxiv

What have you seen on the summits, the peaks that plunge
    their
Icy heads into space? What draws you trembling
To blind altars of rock where man cannot linger
Even in death, where body grows light, and vision
Ranging those uninhabitable stations
Dazzled and emulous among the rage of summoning
Shadows and clouds, may lead you in an instant
Out from all footing? What thread of music, what word in
That frozen silence that drowns the noise of our living?

What is life, you answer,
But to extend life, press its limits farther
Into the uncolonized nothing we must prey on
For every hard-won thought, all new creation
Of stone bronze music words; only at life's limit
Can man reach through necessity and custom
And move self by self into the province
Of that unrealized nature that awaits him,
His own to enter. But there are none to guide
Across the threshold, interpret the saying of perilous
Music or word struck from that quivering climate,
Whose white inquisitors in close attendance
Are pain and madness and annihilation.

XXX

Thistle, briar, thorn:
Dark sayings of an earth
Austere even in the joy
That gave them birth.

Sweet across snow, over rock,
Singing briar that sows
Mountain and desert with alms
Of poverty's rose;

Outlaw thistle, quick
Through wild and ploughed to run
With barbed defiant crest
Bowing to none;

And thorn, weaving in air
Thirsty nets of pain,
Pointed with seed-pearl flowers'
Compassionate rain—

How shall I read your tongue's
Gnomic economy,
To whom the muse of silence
Made the word free?

Be my companions still
With wind and star and stone
Till in your desert music
I hear my own.

Ambulando

i

In middle life when the skin slackens
Its loving clasp of our loose volumes,
When the bone tree stiffens and its well-jointed branches
Begin to creak, to droop a little,
May the spirit hold out no longer for
Old impossible terms, demanding
Rent-free futures where all, all is ripeness,
But cry pax to its equivocal nature and stretch
At ease with wry destiny,
Supple as wind bowing in every reed.

ii

Now that the young with interest no longer
Look on me as one of themselves
Whom they might wish to know or to touch,
Seeing merely another sapless greyhead,
The passport of that disguise conducts me
Through any company unquestioned,
In cool freedom to come and go
With mode and movement, wave and wind.

iii

Communicate with stones, trees, water
If you must vent a heart too full.
Who will hear you now, your words falling
As foreign as bird-tongue
On ears attuned to different vibrations?
Trees, water, stones:
Let these answer a gaze contemplative
Of all things that flow out from them
And back to enter them again.

iv

I do not know the shape of the world.
I cannot set boundaries to experience.
I know it may open out, enlarged suddenly,
In any direction, to unpredictable distance,
Subverting climate and cosmography,
And carrying me far from tried moorings
So that I see myself no more
Under some familiar guise
Resting static as in a photograph,
Nor move as I supposed I was moving
From fixed point to point;
But rock outwards like the last stars that signal
At the frontiers of light,
Fleeing the centre without destination.

Physics of Love

The mutual magnetism of love
Nullifies every other force
That acts upon two infected bodies.
Even gravity is weakened as
They leap obstacles, ride
On their commonest occasions
Six inches above the unbelieving ground.

No Reparation

To make reparation for love so blindly rejected—
How, Gods? how?
After the years have marked them, outward and inwardly,
And they who might have been one remain still two.

Ask pardon for blindness?—well, it argues
A saving recognition, self-knowledge at last,
Although too late to alter what's done, repair
The ravaging of grief, melt the heart's frost.

And that exultant blaze of power that should
Have brought them side to side in matched passion—
Has it gone underground for ever? or smouldered away
Feeding on sour blood for its sole portion?

Ask neither pardon nor forgetfulness,
Do not hope to explain, say no word;
Only be slower to judge now, readier to understand
Those who are not yet dead.

Cry Mercy

Getting older, I grow more personal,
Like more, dislike more
And more intensely than ever—
People, customs, the state,
The ghastly status quo,
And myself, black-hearted crow
In the canting off-white feathers.

Long ago I lost sight of
That famous objectivity,
That classic, godlike calm
For which the wise subdue
Their poisonous hot hearts,
Strength of arm and righteous
Tongue, right indignation.

To know all, to bear all
Quietly, without protest,
To bend never breaking,
To live on, live for another
Day, an equable morning—
Is that what men are born for?
Is that best of all?

To each his own way,
For each his particular end.
Judging one another
By inner, private lights
Fortuitous as ourselves,
We leave some other to judge
By impersonal sunlight

Objective, as we hope,
In the after-world, if any,
What we have made of ourselves,

How we have laid out
That miserly talent, gift
Bestowed on us at the start
For the problematical journey.

How shall I make excuse
That I am not with those
Who lost the loving word
In sumps of fear and hate,
Convicts, displaced persons,
Castaways even of hope?
On them too a sun rises:

Any of us may be hunted
Among them any day.
What certainties assure
Another dawn will wake me
Or the galaxy swim on?
To live is to remember
Remembering to forget.

I lay down no law
For myself or my neighbour.
I search for can and must
Along the broken flare-path,
Pitching left and right
Shaken by voices and thunders,
By other lights, by looms
Of chaos, and my self-shadow.

Liking and disliking,
Unloving and wanting love,
Nearer to, farther from
My cross-grained fellow mortals,
On my level days I cry mercy
And on my lofty days give thanks
For the bewildering rough party.

Wantword

You do not want for words
The words I want
But keep your end up
Easily, with the rest
Having an end to keep.
Words will not serve me so
It is I must run for them
To their ends, having no
End that is not theirs,
Personal affairs
Nor business in company.
You ask words of me
At the wrong hour, in the wrong
Wind, the wrong words.
But when you are not present
Words well up in me
Gesturing, calling
Not to you, not to me
But on my lips, wantword,
Solely to their task
Theirs, mine,
Word-task only.

Man Missing

Someone else, I see,
Will be having the last word about me,
Friend, enemy, or lover
Or gimlet-eyed professor.
Each will think he is true
To the man he thinks he knew
Or knows, he thinks, from the book.
Each will say, Look!

Here he is, to the life,
On my hook or knife;
And each, no doubt, having caught me
Will deal with me plainly, shortly
And as justly as he can
With such a slippery no-man.

Well, I'll be quite curious,
Watching among the dubious
Dead, to see what they make
Of this antique: Genuine, or Fake?
Myself, I've hardly a clue;
I know how I feel, what I do,
But how true my feelings are
And why I perform a particular
Act is quite beyond me,
Analyse and prod me
As I will, as they will,
Nothing quite fills the bill;
And the man writing this now
Is gone as he makes his bow.

Gone, for I never can bind
My seesaw will or mind
That keeps changing with the weather,
Not only from bad to better
And back, but changing aim
And course, myself still the same,
And looking everywhere
I find no centre anywhere,
No real self, only a sort
Of unthought self-conscious thought;
A house with no one at home,
Where any visitor is welcome
To name, try, spare or pan
A genuinely missing no-man.

Ergo Sum

Pretences, discontents—
Leaves of my raging tree,
Self-hate and self-deceit,
All shameful rancours that
Loathing cannot disown,
It is you keep me warm
In the chill fever of
Mood-modes I must try on,
Daily, hourly practising.

To make, unmake, remake,
Unmask and discover,
To cloak, bluff and confess,
These are the ritual
Twistings and contortions
That bedevil relations
Of one, two, and many
In self's game of self-will
In pursuit of its living.

Self scatters itself in
A swarm of witnesses
Against itself, and is
Stronger being scattered
In many that attest
By question, evasion,
Self-confirming doubt, all
Continuities that
Are covert forms of growing.

I die therefore I am:
Dying out of myself,
Dying into myself,
Sieved and sea-changed through
The calendar of roles,

Disguises, feints, black-outs,
Worn down by treadmill thoughts,
Torn by the harrow
And heartburn of becoming.

Who am I to command
A self and its leaf-selves
Living dispersed through all
With the salt grains of the sea?
I follow, obeying a word
That leads in whirling dance
Through the cloud of days
And the cries of living and dead
To the last leaf-burning.

Open the Heart

To run a thousand miles from a thousand men,
Flinching from every face indifferent or hostile,

Masks you cannot compose a mask to meet—
Doesn't it still leave you where you started,

Heart pounding because you could not endure
To catch your face naked in the mirror

And see heart, face, the whole quivering self
No more than a puff of wind

Raising the dust, settling into dust——?
No no no, that's mere

Decoration, rationalization, still running away—
Simply, you dare not stand, because

To speak out is more desperate than to keep silence,
To open the heart is to bleed to death surely.

94

BASIL DOWLING

Through a Glass, Darkly

Though spacious lands and oceans and far skies,
  My head sees from its five-feet-something shelf,
No matter how it tries
    It cannot clearly, wholly see itself;
And if it could, might hardly recognize,
  Since cameras and mirrors can tell lies.

So it may be with death, the pictured terror.
  That thronged, yet solitary frontier station
May, when the pilgrim turns discoverer,
    Bring such a revelation
As will unhide the hugeness of our error,
  Beyond life's luminous, distorting mirror.

Scything

All day I swing my level scythe,
  Slow-marching on the severed swath;
Content to know myself alone
    With grass, and leaves, and gusty sun.

The random handle that I hold,
  A strong lopped bough, bone-dry, and curled,
Is emblem of an ancient time
    When wandering man first dreamed of home.

Scared by my near blade's foreign hiss
  A lizard flickers where I pass
Like Adam stooping to the ground
    With a lost Eden in his mind.

Halfwit

He walks with shopping basket, and an air
    Of some tremendous secret in his keeping,
He dodges obstacles that are not there;
    Now checks his pace, and now goes skipping, leaping.
A noise frets in his head; he lets it loose
    And hears it flit about him like a bat;
Hoot of an owl, or trumpet of a goose:
    Then no one passes and he lifts his hat.
Shopping he goes, and might, with his poor head,
    Bring stones and scorpions for meat and bread.

Mushrooms

We went to look for stragglers on a ridge
Beyond the upland pasture, where the rough
Scrub country rolled away. But what we saw,
Or what I now remember was near home
Beside the neat green oatfield, a score or so
Mushrooms among the daisies and dandelions
And dewy wine-red sorrel, like a flock
Of sheep and lambs looked down on from a height;
Domes of old vellum, and buttons coy and small
White as new gloves; and scattered here and there
Some kicked by cows, showing their fleshy gills.
That morning we walked far and soaked our boots
Along the wet sheep-tracks, but now my thoughts
Stay in that mushroom paddock to recover
Childhood and all sweet mornings, dew, and grass.

The Trapped Hare

This morning I found a hare gaoled alive in a gin,
One red forepaw held bitten in clenched iron.
With ears laid back and large eyes full of woe
He crouched on the scoured floor of his open prison
Resting, poor creature, and gathering strength for his struggle.
Set him free, urged my heart, but my mind made excuse
As it will often at sight of familiar wrong.
My hollow sophistry said, End his pain—
Better to enter life maimed, pleaded those eyes.
So I dallied too long between thinking and doing
Until the practical farmer came without scruple.
Then the hoarse feminine scream and spinal blow
And the limp body dangling downward dishonoured;
Sagacity brought low and swiftness stilled
By braggart jaws set wicked in a gap.
There will be other hares, but never this one seen
Glad in his freedom some sweet evening
Skirting a boundary with easy idle stride,
Or squatting lord of his hundred-acre domain,
Hind legs like skis and tall ears up
And coat of ruddier brown than ripened corn.
No more, no more, this beauty and wild grace,
And I go sadly, troubled with grief and guilt
That I stood by, a dumb witness consenting
To the murder of an exquisite work of God.

The Unreturning Native

Above the sounds that echo eerily
    Still in my mind
I hear those Valkyries of wild sea-wind,
    Though now they blow more kind.

Of all lost faces one remains with me,
    The downcast face
Of that dark, woebegone, uprooted race;
    But now it haunts me less.

That raw harsh landscape in my memory
    Once seemed hostile,
But tones more truthfully with human ill
    Than gentle vale and hill.

Old friends beloved and loving faithfully
    There yet abide,
To press their soft assault upon that pride
    Which even from love would hide.

Still may that love, that land, and that blown sea,
    Though never again
Present to prick my heart and eyes, remain
    As constant as my pain.

CHARLES SPEAR

O Matre Pulchra . . .

When you whom Jules de Goncourt's prose
Had placed on shallow, leaf-strewn steps,
Against a tower, slate-roofed and rose,
When you gaze in your mirror's depths,

Dear worldling, do you understand
My seeing in those raffish eyes,
Instead of ladies of the land,
My landlord's fancy lady rise?

The Disinherited

They cared for nothing but the days and hours
Of freedom, and in silent scorn
Ignored the worldly watchers and the powers,
Left staples shattered and uptorn,
Filed window-bars and dynamited towers.

What was their wisdom whom no vice could hold?
Remote as any gipsy rover,
They stared along the cliffs, mauve fold on fold,
And watched the bees fly over.

From velvet hills, trees in the river-bed,
From glassy reefs in skeins of foam,
They reared the shell of vision and of words unsaid
To be their haunting and their earthly home.

Memoriter

Ovals of opal on dislustred seas,
Skyshine, and all that indolent afternoon
No clash of arms, no shouting on the breeze;
Only the reeds moaned soft or high their empty rune.

The paladins played chess and did not care,
The crocus pierced the turf with random dart.
Then twanged a cord. Through space, from Oultremer
That other arrow veered towards your heart.

Christoph

The wind blew strongly like the voice of fate
Through cheerless sunlight, and the black yawl strained
And creaked across the sullen slate
Of Zuider Zee. That night it rained;

The Hook of Holland drenched in diamonds lay
Far southward; but the exile coming home
Turns back to hours like golden tissues stacked away,
And sees no more the sulky, weltering foam,
But only roses, or white honey in the comb.

At a Danse Macabre

The glittering topaz in your glass
Was vintaged forty years ago;
Your emerald has seen eight kings pass,
A thousand thousand candles glow.

Watched in a jewel, the taper curls;
The royal men, the wine that flows
Are tints and crowns; the peerless girls
Are broken shadows of a rose.

Environs of Vanholt I

White and blue, an outspread fan,
The sea slopes to the Holmcliff, and the dawn
Spins vaporous spokes across the Broken Span
To light up Razor Drop and Winesael Yawn.

Beanpod sleeps out beside his malt-filled pot;
Behind him lies the still and silver land;
No atom bomb drops from a shapely hand,
But birds of boding in a greasy knot
Pick at the rusted corpse half-hid in sand.

The Prisoner

I walked along the winding road;
It was high summer; on one side
Behind pale foliage sinuously flowed
The hand-sown wheat in rustling pride.

Grey sprawling stone, before me towered the school;
I touched the chapel-corner through the hedge,
Traced dimly in the window's painted pool
Three mitres and the shield with rope and wedge.

Deep peace! Yet there was panic terror shut inside;
The bronze bells rolled and reeled in flowing tide.
Against that shock time buckled to resist,
And no sound pierced the loneliness, no voices cried;
Only the great towers trembled in the pouring mist.

Karl

Outside among the talking criss-cross reeds
The night of rain; then from the south
The whisper softly growing that none heeds
At first, till it comes weaving with a giant's mouth;

Till through the pass the hissing torches stream
Under the steely arrows of the rain,
And cavalry and foot and sweating team
Check at the ford and then surge on again.

The heralds in the Gothic Saxon blue
Come spurring, and the levelled trumpets sing.
Then in the courtyard clamour: cracked bells ring
Like waterfalls, and the exultant host pours through
The shattered hall to claim its exiled king.

News from Paris

Down through Venetian blinds the morning air
Sifts from a sky where peach and azure fuse;
Street noises enter too, and in a distant square
A regimental band plays *Sambre et Meuse*.

It is Felicity: she sits and reads once more
The Gothic script of the West-Easterly Divan;
Her silver shoe just touches the waxed floor,
And pot pourri transcends the vase from old Japan.

Animae Superstiti

Some leagues into that land I too have fared;
The diligence along the causeway sped,
While from the left a giant planet glared
Across the restless marsh with face of lead.

In number we were four: you, child, and I;
The swordsman next, who wore his mocking air
Of Papal Zouave, fencing master, spy,
And last the golliwog with vacant, saxe-blue stare.

Onward we whirled; you slept disturbed in mind,
And from your hand the English roses fell;
Europe by lamplight far behind,
We clove the white fog's shifting swell.

So for an hour, and then I must return,
And you with your creatures ply insensate flight.
Broken I stood beneath the frontier light,
Till through the endless marsh I could discern
No wheels, no sound, only the airs of night.

Scott-Moncrieff's Beowulf

In the curdled afterglow of night
The long ship leaves the cliff, the ness, the cave;
Unending arcs of icy light
Flicker about her on the climbing wave;

And coming close fierce warriors crowd
To shout across the Swan's Way. See! They pass.
She drives through trailing veils of cloud,
And time pours down like rain on weeping glass.

From a Book of Hours

Bearing white myrrh and incense, autumn melts
Through flower and fruit and combed blonde straw;
Thunder looms on the mountain forest-belt;
The winter firewood purrs beneath the saw.

Our garden scents upbillow like the veils
Of Solomon's Temple, shimmer in the rain,
And all is peace. Slowly the daylight fails,
And voice and lute bring back the stars again.

1894 in London

Like torn-up newsprint the nonchalant snow
Creaked down incessantly on Red Lion Square.
Clock chimes were deadbeats. Clang! Nowhere to go!
The cabbies drove with marble stare,
The snowed-up statues had a pensive air.

Inside the pub the spirits flowed,
And Sal and Kate the guardees' tanners shared;
Out in the dusk the newsboys crowed,
And to infinity the lamp-posts flared,
The gas-blue lilies of the Old Kent Road.

Old England's blue hour of unmeasured nips,
The Quiet Time for Dorian Gray,
The day off for the barmaid's hips,
Prayer-Book revision time down Lambeth way.

Karl

All day he stood at Weeping Cross,
While with its shot-ripped flags and battered train,
In full retreat, and stunned by loss,
The army came back through the freezing rain.

Behind, the rearguard seemed to swirl and drown,
As the gunsmoke curdled through the pass.
The slamming volleys switched the wet leaves down,
And scythed the dead upon the reddened grass.

Have done! Let none hereafter heed this cry
For the apostolic chivalry of time long past;
This prayer of all that smote the marble sky
Is least, and yet the proudest, for it is the last.

God Save the Stock

Dusk falters over shelf and chair,
Carnation webs of shadows hold
A symbol in that tranquil air,
A candle's hoop of uncoined gold.

He writes reports in sweet repose—
The Jews require new management;
Korea soothed with flowing prose,
He writes in charmed astonishment.

The horn-rimmed prefect on the primrose path
Commands success with lip upcurled.
Fare well, Commander of the Bath,
And good luck, playboy of the western world!

Balthasar

Hid near a lily-spangled stream,
The wild duck smooths his satin breast;
A league back, shattered hauberks gleam;
The wall no longer guards the West.

The crystal willow boughs of spring
Shimmer above on pearl-shell skies,
And Balthasar sets signet-ring
To war-dispatches full of lies.

Promised Land

Dispart the frost-white boughs, and lo!
The world of winter, mile on mile;
Wind-wavy seas of unplumbed snow,
Then endless peaks and one defile.

The high elect would fear to cross
Those wastes unconquerable, ideal:
There lies your path; count all as loss,
Cast armour by, lay down your steel;

For you shall walk the sheer gulf's brink,
Through glass-blue caves all brittle spars
And flaws. Thereafter you shall sink,
Snowblind in slush, beneath the stars.

Joachim of Flora

A swathe of violet at break of day,
Ribbon of glory for the opening reign;
And red and yellow like the flag of Spain
The fishing-boats at sea again
Through sheets of glitter drew away.

He left the sands by Dunkerque Lane
And watched the birds attend in solemn file
The ploughman as he clove with might and main
The path of honour and the line of style;

So putting by his craven doubt
He vowed to clasp and kiss the fleeting hour
While all the bells for joy rang out
Four-in-hand harmonies from spire and tower.

Escape

Against deep seas blue-black like mussel-shells
The island arched its bluffs and stony scarps,
Which, wave-rocked, tolled in winter time like bells,
Or chimed to spring as sweet as Irish harps.

Above, a fool's crown of canary cloud,
Moulded by mighty winds to dizzy height,
Leaned to the isle like press of sail o'erbowed,
And sunshine pierced the eyes with swords of light.

This have we chosen, far from friends and home,
This space of barren rock and crimson heath,
With cliffs of quaking honey-comb
And the tides of death in the galleries beneath.

Environs of Vanholt II

See! In the troubled glow of dawn
World rising—mountain to lowland smoothly laid,
River and hedgerow sharply drawn;
It is the continent of shade.

Sail into Stonecliff next; heraldic bronze
Chrysanthemums turn to the moody sea.
We call your name; there will be no response;
Only a dog barks in this land of memory.

ALLEN CURNOW

Time

I am the nor'west air nosing among the pines
I am the water-race and the rust on railway lines
I am the mileage recorded on the yellow signs.

I am dust, I am distance, I am lupins along the beach
I am the sums the sole-charge teachers teach
I am cows called to milking and the magpie's screech.

I am nine o'clock in the morning when the office is clean
I am the slap of the belting and the smell of the machine
I am the place in the park where the lovers were seen.

I am recurrent music the children hear
I am level noises in the remembering ear
I am the sawmill and the passionate second gear.

I, Time, am all these yet these exist
Among my mountainous fabrics like a mist,
So do they the measurable world resist.

I, Time, call down, condense, confer
On the willing memory the shape these were:
I, more than your conscious carrier,

Am island, am sea, am father, farm, and friend;
Though I am here all things my coming attend;
I am, you have heard it, the Beginning and the End.

House and Land

Wasn't this the site, asked the historian,
Of the original homestead?
Couldn't tell you, said the cowman;
I just live here, he said,
Working for old Miss Wilson
Since the old man's been dead.

Moping under the bluegums
The dog trailed his chain
From the privy as far as the fowlhouse
And back to the privy again,
Feeling the stagnant afternoon
Quicken with the smell of rain.

There sat old Miss Wilson,
With her pictures on the wall,
The baronet uncle, mother's side,
And one she called The Hall;
Taking tea from a silver pot
For fear the house might fall.

People in the *colonies*, she said,
Can't quite understand . . .
Why, from Waiau to the mountains
It was all father's land.

She's all of eighty said the cowman,
Down at the milking-shed.
I'm leaving here next winter.
Too bloody quiet, he said.

The spirit of exile, wrote the historian,
Is strong in the people still.
He reminds me rather, said Miss Wilson,
Of Harriet's youngest, Will.

The cowman, home from the shed, went drinking
With the rabbiter home from the hill.

The sensitive nor'west afternoon
Collapsed, and the rain came;
The dog crept into his barrel
Looking lost and lame.
But you can't attribute to either
Awareness of what great gloom
Stands in a land of settlers
With never a soul at home.

The Unhistoric Story

Whaling for continents coveted deep in the south
The Dutchman envied the unknown, drew bold
Images of market-place, populous river-mouth,
The Land of Beach ignorant of the value of gold:
    Morning in Murderers' Bay,
    Blood drifted away.
    It was something different, something
    Nobody counted on.

Spider, clever and fragile, Cook showed how
To spring a trap for islands, turning from planets
His measuring mission, showed what the musket could do,
Made his Christmas goose of the wild gannets.
    Still as the collier steered
    No continent appeared;
    It was something different, something
    Nobody counted on.

The roving tentacles touched, rested, clutched
Substantial earth, that is, accustomed haven
For the hungry whaler. Some inland, some hutched
Rudely in bays, the shaggy foreshore shaven,

Lusted, preached as they knew;
But as the children grew
It was something different, something
Nobody counted on.

Green slashed with flags, pipeclay and boots in the bush,
Christ in canoes and the musketed Maori boast;
All a rubble-rattle at Time's glacial push:
Vogel and Seddon howling empire from an empty coast
    A vast ocean laughter
    Echoed unheard, and after
    All it was different, something
    Nobody counted on.

The pilgrim dream pricked by a cold dawn died
Among the chemical farmers, the fresh towns; among
Miners, not husbandmen, who piercing the side
Let the land's life, found like all who had so long
    Bloodily or tenderly striven
    To rearrange the given,
    It was something different, something
    Nobody counted on.

After all re-ordering of old elements
Time trips up all but the humblest of heart
Stumbling after the fire, but not in the smoke of events;
For many are called, but many are left at the start,
    And whatever islands may be
    Under or over the sea,
    It is something different, something
    Nobody counted on.

Wild Iron

Sea go dark, dark with wind,
Feet go heavy, heavy with sand,
Thoughts go wild, wild with the sound
Of iron on the old shed swinging, clanging:
Go dark, go heavy, go wild, go round,
    Dark with the wind,
    Heavy with the sand,
Wild with the iron that tears at the nail
And the foundering shriek of the gale.

Sailing or Drowning

In terms of some green myth, sailing or drowning,
Each day makes clear a statement to the next;
But to make out our tomorrow from its motives
Is pure guessing, yesterday's were so mixed.

Papa, Atea, parents of gods or islands,
Quickly forgave the treacherous beaches, none
So bloodily furrowed that the secret tides
Could not make the evening and the morning one.

Ambition has annulled that constitution;
In the solid sea and the space over the sea
Explosions of a complex origin
Shock, rock, and split the memory.

Sailing or drowning, the living and the dead,
Less than the gist of what has just been said.

Out of Sleep

Awake but not yet up, too early morning
Brings you like bells in matrix of mist
Noises the mind may finger, but no meaning.
Two blocks away a single car has crossed

Your intersection with the hour; each noise
A cough in the cathedral of your waking—
The cleaners have no souls, no sins—each does
Some job, Christ dying or the day breaking.

This you suppose is what goes on all day.
No one is allowed long to stop and listen,
But takes brief turns at it: now as you lie

Dead calm, a gust in the damp cedar hissing
Will have the mist right off in half a minute.
You will not grasp the meaning, you will be in it.

The Old Provincial Council Buildings, Christchurch

The steps are saucered in the trodden parts,
But that doesn't take long to happen here;
Two or three generations' traffic starts
In stone like this to make time's meaning clear.

Azaleas burn your gaze away below,
Corbel and finial tell you where to stop;
For present purposes, it does to know
Transport is licensed somewhere at the top.

Children of those who suffered a sea change
May wonder how much history was quarried
And carted, hoisted, carved; and find it strange
How shallow here their unworn age lies buried

Before its time, before their time, whose eyes
Get back from a stopped clock their own surprise.

The Skeleton of the Great Moa
in the Canterbury Museum,
Christchurch

The skeleton of the moa on iron crutches
Broods over no great waste; a private swamp
Was where this tree grew feathers once, that hatches
Its dusty clutch, and guards them from the damp.

Interesting failure to adapt on islands,
Taller but not more fallen than I, who come
Bone to his bone, peculiarly New Zealand's.
The eyes of children flicker round this tomb

Under the skylights, wonder at the huge egg
Found in a thousand pieces, pieced together
But with less patience than the bones that dug
In time deep shelter against ocean weather:

Not I, some child, born in a marvellous year,
Will learn the trick of standing upright here.

Landfall in Unknown Seas

*The 300th Anniversary of the Discovery of New Zealand
by Abel Tasman, 13 December 1642*

I

Simply by sailing in a new direction
You could enlarge the world.
                      You picked your captain,
Keen on discoveries, tough enough to make them,
Whatever vessels could be spared from other
More urgent service for a year's adventure;
Took stock of the more probable conjectures
About the Unknown to be traversed, all
Guesses at golden coasts and tales of monsters
To be digested into plain instructions
For likely and unlikely situations.

All this resolved and done, you launched the whole
On a fine morning, the best time of year,
Skies widening and the oceanic furies
Subdued by summer illumination; time
To go and to be gazed at going
On a fine morning, in the Name of God
Into the nameless waters of the world.

O you had estimated all the chances
Of business in those waters, the world's waters
Yet unexploited.
                But more than the sea-empire's
Cannon, the dogs of bronze and iron barking
From Timor to the Straits, backed up the challenge.
Between you and the South an older enmity
Lodged in the searching mind, that would not tolerate
So huge a hegemony of ignorance.

There, where your Indies had already sprinkled
Their tribes like ocean rains, you aimed your voyage;
Like them invoked your God, gave seas to history
And islands to new hazardous tomorrows.

II

Suddenly exhilaration
Went off like a gun, the whole
Horizon, the long chase done,
Hove to. There was the seascape
Crammed with coast, surprising
As new lands will, the sailor
Moving on the face of the waters,
Watching the earth take shape
Round the unearthly summits, brighter
Than its emerging colour.

Yet this, no far fool's errand,
Was less than the heart desired,
In its old Indian dream
The glittering gulfs ascending
Past palaces and mountains
Making one architecture.
Here the uplifted structure,
Peak and pillar of cloud—
O splendour of desolation—reared
Tall from the pit of the swell,
With a shadow, a finger of wind, forbade
Hopes of a lucky landing.

Always to islanders danger
Is what comes over the sea;
Over the yellow sands and the clear
Shallows, the dull filament
Flickers, the blood of strangers:
Death discovered the Sailor

O in a flash, in a flat calm,
A clash of boats in the bay
And the day marred with murder.
The dead required no further
Warning to keep their distance;
The rest, noting the failure,
Pushed on with a reconnaissance
To the north; and sailed away.

III

Well, home is the Sailor, and that is a chapter
In a schoolbook, a relevant yesterday
We thought we knew all about, being much apter
    To profit, sure of our ground,
No murderers mooring in our Golden Bay.

But now there are no more islands to be found
And the eye scans risky horizons of its own
In unsettled weather, and murmurs of the drowned
    Haunt their familiar beaches—
Who navigates us towards what unknown

But not improbable provinces? Who reaches
A future down for us from the high shelf
Of spiritual daring? Not those speeches
    Pinning on the Past like a decoration
For merit that congratulates itself,

O not the self-important celebration
Or most painstaking history, can release
The current of a discoverer's elation
    And silence the voices saying,
'Here is the world's end where wonders cease.'

Only by a more faithful memory, laying
On him the half-light of a diffident glory,
The Sailor lives, and stands beside us, paying
    Out into our time's wave
The stain of blood that writes an island story.

Tomb of an Ancestor

IN MEMORIAM, R.L.M.G.

The oldest of us burst into tears and cried
Let me go home, but she stayed, watching
At her staircase window ship after ship ride
Like birds her grieving sunsets; there sat stitching

Grandchildren's things. She died by the same sea.
High over it she led us in the steepening heat
To the yellow grave; her clay
Chose that way home: dismissed, our feet

Were seen to have stopped and turned again down hill;
The street fell like an ink-blue river
In the heat to the bay, the basking ships, this Isle
Of her oblivion, our broad day. Heaped over

So lightly, she stretched like time behind us, or
Graven in cloud, our farthest ancestor.

Self-portrait

The wistful camera caught this four-year-old
But could not stare him into wistfulness;
He holds the toy that he is given to hold:
A passionate failure or a staled success

Look back into their likeness while I look
With pity not self-pity at the plain
Mechanical image that I first mistook
For my own image; there, timid or vain,

Semblance of my own eyes my eyes discern
Casting on mine as I cast back on these
Regard not self-regard: till the toy turn
Into a lover clasped, into wide seas,

The salt or visionary wave, and the days heap
Sorrow upon sorrow for all he could not keep.

Eden Gate

The paper boat sank to the bottom of the garden
The train steamed in at the white wicked gate,
The old wind wished in the hedge, the sodden
Sack loved the yellow shoot;

And scampering children woke the world
Singing Happy Doomsday over all the green willows
That sprang like panic from the crotch of the cold
Sappy earth, and away in the withered hollows

A hand no warmer than a cloud rummaged
At the river's roots: up there in the sky
God's one blue eye looked down on the damaged
Boy tied by the string of a toy

And saw him off at the gate and the train
All over again.

Unhurt, There is No Help

When was it first they called each other mine?
Not in Donne's day: by then their love had grown
Or shrunk from Phoenix into spider, sign
Of sinner turned addict. Love, be your own

And stay the far side of that Tree
Whose seed struck earth between us; give again
A bite of apple; do not mind if He
Is somewhere in the garden, or that pain

Is frost or blight and the leaf blackens.
That is your birthright and redeeming sin.
Unhurt, there is no help for her who wakens
Puzzled, her sole power gone, in the obscene

Daffodil bed where the decrepit knees
Promised speech from heaven, and could barely please.

The Waking Bird Refutes

Rain's unassuaging fountains multiply
In air on earth and leaf. The Flood began
This way, listened to at windows by
The sleepless: one wept, one revolved a plan,

One died and rose again, one felt
That colder breath blow from the poles of lip
At love's meridian. This way now the spoilt
Firmament of the blood dissolves and drops;

The bright waste repossessive element
Beats barely audible, one sound imposing
Silence upon silence. This way I went
To pull our histories down, down, heavens accusing

Of rainbowed guile, whose penal rains descend.
But the waking bird refutes: world will not end.

To Forget Self and All

To forget self and all, forget foremost
This whimpering second unlicked self my country,
To go like nobody's fool an ungulled ghost
By unadorned midnight and the pitch of noon
Commanding at large everywhere his entry,
Unimaginable waterchinks, granular dark of a stone?
Why that'd be freedom heyday, hey
For freedom that'd be the day
And as good a dream as any to be damned for.

Then to patch it up with self and all and all
This tousled sunny-mouthed sandy-legged coast,
These painted and these rusted streets,
This heart so supple and small,
Blinding mountain, deafening river
And smooth anxious sheets,
And go like a sober lover like nobody's ghost?
Why that'd be freedom heyday, hey
Freedom! That'd be the day
And as good a dream as any to be damned to.

To sink both self and all why sink the whole
Phenomenal enterprise, colours shapes and sizes
Low like Lucifer's bolt from the cockshied roost
Of groundless paradise: peeled gold gull
Whom the cracked verb of his thoughts
Blew down blew up mid-air, where the sea's gorge rises,
The burning brain's nine feathering fathom doused
And prints with bubbles one grand row of noughts?
Why that'd be freedom heyday, hey
For freedom, that'd be the day
And as good a dream as any to be damned by.

Elegy on My Father

Tremayne Curnow, of Canterbury, New Zealand, 1880–1949

Spring in his death abounds among the lily islands,
There to bathe him for the grave antipodean snows
Fall floodlong, rivermouths all in bloom, and those
Fragile church timbers quiver
By the bourne of his burial where robed he goes
No journey at all. One sheet's enough to cover
My end of the world and his, and the same silence.

While in Paddington autumn is air-borne, earth-given,
Day's nimbus nearer staring, colder smoulders;
Breath of a death not my own bewilders
Dead calm with breathless choirs
O bird-creation singing where the world moulders!
God's poor, the crutched and stunted spires
Thumb heavenward humorously under the unriven

Marble November has nailed across their sky:
Up there, dank ceiling is the dazzling floor
All souls inhabit, the lilied seas, no shore
My tear-smudged map mislimned.
When did a wind of the extreme South before
Mix autumn, spring, and death? False maps are dimmed,
Lovingly they mock each other, image and eye.

The ends of the earth are folded in his grave
In sound of the Pacific and the hills he tramped singing,
God knows romantically or by what love bringing
Wine from a clay creek-bed,
Good bread; or by what glance the inane skies ringing
Lucidly round; or by what shuffle or tread
Warning the dirt of miracles. Still that nave

He knelt in puts off its poor planks, looms loftier
Lonelier than Losinga's that spells in stone
The Undivided Name. *Oh quickening bone*
Of the Mass-priest under grass
Green in my absent spring, sweet relic atone
To our earth's Lord for the pride of all our voyages,
That the salt winds which scattered us blow softer.

London, November 1949

The Eye is More or Less Satisfied with Seeing

Wholehearted he can't move
From where he is, nor love

Wholehearted that place,
Indigene janus-face,

Half mocking half,
Neither caring to laugh.

Does true or false sun rise?
Do both half eyes tell lies?

Cradle or grave, which view's
The actual of the two?

Half eyes foretell, forget
Sunrise, sunset,

Or closed a fraction's while
Half eyes half smile

Upon light the spider lid
Snares, holds hid

And holds him whole (between
The split scarves of that scene)

Brimming astride a pulse
Of moon-described eyeball's

Immobile plenitude—
Flower of the slight stemmed flood.

Snap open! He's all eyes, wary,
Darting both ways one query,

Whether the moonbeam glanced
Upon half to whole enhanced,

Or wholly the soul's error
And confederate mirror.

Keep in a Cool Place

A bee in a bloom on the long hand of a floral
Clock can't possibly tell the right time
And if it could whatever would the poor bee do with it
In insufferably hot weather like this?

Everything white looks washed, at the correct distance
And may be the correct distance. You could eat
Our biggest ship sweet as sugar and space can make her.
Every body's just unwrapped, one scrap of a shaving

Left for luck or the look, the maker's seal intact,
Glad to be genuine! The glassy seaside's
Exact to the last detail, tick of a tide,
Fluke of the wind, slant of a sail. The swimmers

On lawns and the athletes in cosy white beds have visitors
And more flowers. Poor bee! He can make up time
At frantic no speed, whether tick or tock,
Hour or minute hand's immaterial. That's

Exactly how it is now. It is. It is
Summer all over the striped humming-top of the morning
And what lovely balloons, prayer-filled (going up!) to fluke
For once and for all the right time, the correct distance.

Jack-in-the-Boat

*is always ready to row across the bath or lake. Wind up the
motor, and watch him dip his blades like a true oarsman—
in, out, in, out—with never-tiring enthusiasm.*
                        —LEGEND ON A TOY-MAKER'S PACKAGE

Children, children, come and look
Through the crack in the corner of the middle of the world
At the clockwork man in a cardboard house.
He's crying, children, crying.
    He's not true, really.

Once he was new like you, you see
Through the crack in the corner of the middle of the night,
The bright blue man on the wind-up sea,
Oh, he went so beautifully.
    He's not true, really.

O cruel was the pleasure-land they never should have painted
On the front and the back, the funny brand of weather,
For the crack in the corner of the middle of the picture
Let the colours leak away.
    He's not true, really.

126

One at a time, children, come and look
Through the crack in the corner in the middle of the day
At Jack-in-the-Boat where the light leaves float.
He's dying of a broken spring.
    He's not true, really.

Spectacular Blossom

Mock up again, summer, the sooty altars
Between the sweltering tides and the tin gardens,
All the colours of the stained bow windows.
Quick, she'll be dead on time, the single
Actress shuffling red petals to this music,
Percussive light! So many suns she harbours
And keeps them jigging, her puppet suns,
All over the dead hot calm impure
Blood noon tide of the breathless day.

Are the victims always so beautiful?

Pearls pluck at her, she has tossed her girls
Breast-flowers for keepsakes now she is going
For ever and astray. I see her feet
Slip into the perfect fit the shallows make her
Purposefully, sure as she is the sea
Levels its lucent ruins underfoot
That were sharp dead white shells, that will be sands.
The shallows kiss like knives.

Always for this
They are chosen for their beauty.

Wristiest slaughterman December smooths
The temple bones and parts the grey-blown brows
With humid fingers. It is an ageless wind
That loves with knives, it knows our need, it flows
Justly, simply as water greets the blood,
And woody tumours burst in scarlet spray.
An old man's blood spills bright as a girl's
On beaches where the knees of light crash down.
These dying ejaculate their bloom.

Can anyone choose
And call it beauty?—The victims
Are always beautiful.

He Cracked a Word

He cracked a word to get at the inside
Of the inside, then the whole paper bag full
The man said were ripe and good.
The shrunken kernels
Like black tongues in dead mouths derided
The sillinesses of song and wagging wisdom:
These made a small dumb pile, the hopping shells
Froze to the floor, and those made patterns
Half-witted cameras glared at, finding as usual
Huge meteorites in mouseland.
What barefaced robbery!
He sat, sat, sat mechanically adding
To the small dumb pile, to the patterns on the floor,
Conscious of nothing but memories, wishes,
And a faint but unmistakable pricking of the thumbs,
The beginnings of his joy.

A Small Room with Large Windows

i

What it would look like if really there were only
One point of the compass not known illusory,
All other quarters proving nothing but quaint
Obsolete expressions of truth north (would it be?),
And seeds, birds, children, loves, and thoughts bore down
The unwinding abiding beam from birth
To death! What a plan!
                              Or parabola.
You describe yours, I mine, simple as that,
With a pop and a puff of nonchalant stars up top,
Then down, dutiful dead stick, down
(True north all the way nevertheless).

One way to save space and a world of trouble.

A word on arrival, a word on departure.
A passage of proud verse, rightly construed.
An unerring pen to edit the ensuing silences
(That's more like it).

ii

                    Seven ageing pine trees hide
Their heads in air but, planted on bare knees,
Supplicate wind and tide. See if you can
See it (if this is it), half earth, half heaven,
Half land, half water, what you call a view
Strung out between the windows and the tree trunks;
Below sills a world moist with new making where
The mangrove race number their cheated floods.
Now in a field azure rapidly folding
Swells a cloud sable, a bad bitching squall
Thrashes the old pines, has them twitching
Root and branch, rumouring a Götterdämmerung.

Foreknowledge infects them to the heart.

Comfortable

To creak in tune, comfortable to damn
Slime-suckled mangrove for its muddy truckling
With time and tide, knotted to the vein it leeches.

iii

In the interim, how the children should be educated,
Pending a decision, a question much debated
In our island realms. It being, as it is,
Out of the question merely to recognize
The whole three hundred and sixty degrees,
Which prudence if not propriety forbids,
It is necessary to avail oneself of aids
Like the Bible, or no Bible, free swimming tuition,
Art, sex, no sex and so on. Not to direct
So much as to normalize personality, protect
From all hazards of climate, parentage, diet,
Whatever it is exists. While, on the quiet,
It is understood there is a judgement preparing
Which finds the compass totally without bearing
And the present course correct beyond a doubt,
There being two points precisely, one in, one out.

iv

A kingfisher's naked arc alight
Upon a dead stick in the mud
A scarlet geranium wild on a wet bank
A man stepping it out in the near distance
With a dog and a bag

on a spit of shell
On a wire in a mist

a gannet impacting
Explode a dozen diverse dullnesses
Like a burst of accurate fire.

130

DENIS GLOVER

Holiday Piece

Now let my thoughts be like the Arrow, wherein was gold,
And purposeful like the Kawarau, but not so cold.

Let them sweep higher than the hawk ill-omened,
Higher than peaks perspective-piled beyond Ben Lomond;
Let them be like at evening an Otago sky
Where detonated clouds in calm confusion lie.

Let them be smooth and sweet as all those morning lakes,
Yet active and leaping, like fish the fisherman takes;
And strong as the dark deep-rooted hills, strong
As twilight hours over Lake Wakatipu are long;

And hardy, like the tenacious mountain tussock,
And spacious, like the Mackenzie plain, not narrow;
And numerous, as tourists in Queenstown;
And cheerfully busy, like the gleaning sparrow.

Lastly, that snowfield, visible from Wanaka,
Compound their patience—suns only brighten,
And no rains darken, a whiteness nothing could whiten.

The Magpies

When Tom and Elizabeth took the farm
  The bracken made their bed,
And *Quardle oodle ardle wardle doodle*
  The magpies said.

Tom's hand was strong to the plough
  Elizabeth's lips were red,
And *Quardle oodle ardle wardle doodle*
  The magpies said.

Year in year out they worked
>While the pines grew overhead,
And *Quardle oodle ardle wardle doodle*
>The magpies said.

But all the beautiful crops soon went
>To the mortgage-man instead,
And *Quardle oodle ardle wardle doodle*
>The magpies said.

Elizabeth is dead now (it's years ago)
>Old Tom went light in the head;
And *Quardle oodle ardle wardle doodle*
>The magpies said.

The farm's still there. Mortgage corporations
>Couldn't give it away.
And *Quardle oodle ardle wardle doodle*
>The magpies say.

Songs

I

These songs will not stand—
The wind and the sand will smother.

Not I but another
Will make songs worth the bother:

>The rimu or kauri he,
>I'm but the cabbage tree,

>>*Sings Harry to an old guitar.*

II

If everywhere in the street
Is the indifferent, the accustomed eye
Nothing can elate,
It's nothing to do with me,
    Sings Harry in the wind-break.

To the north are islands like stars
In the blue water
And south, in that crystal air,
The ice-floes grind and mutter,
    Sings Harry in the wind-break.

At one flank old Tasman, the boar,
Slashes and tears,
And the other Pacific's sheer
Mountainous anger devours,
    Sings Harry in the wind-break.

From the cliff-top a boy
Felt that great motion,
And pupil to the horizon's eye
Grew wide with vision,
    Sings Harry in the wind-break.

But grew to own fences barbed
Like the words of a quarrel;
And the sea never disturbed
Him fat as a barrel,
    Sings Harry in the wind-break.

Who once would gather all Pacific
In a net wide as his heart
Soon is content to watch the traffic
Or lake waves breaking short,
    Sings Harry in the wind-break.

Once the Days

Once the days were clear
Like mountains in water,
The mountains were always there
And the mountain water;

And I was a fool leaving
Good land to moulder,
Leaving the fences sagging
And the old man older
To follow my wild thoughts
Away over the hill,
Where there is only the world
And the world's ill,
　　　　　　　sings Harry.

The Casual Man

Come, mint me up the golden gorse,
Mine me the yellow clay
—There's no money in my purse
For a rainy day,
　　　　　　　sings Harry.

My father left me his old coat,
Nothing more than that;
And will my head take hurt
In an old hat?
　　　　　　　sings Harry.

They all concern themselves too much
With what a clock shows.
But does the casual man care
How the world goes?
　　　　　　　sings Harry.

A little here, a little there—
Why should a man worry?
Let the world hurry by,
I'll not hurry,

                              sings Harry.

Thistledown

Once I followed horses
And once I followed whores,
And marched once with a banner
For some great cause,

                              sings Harry.

But that was thistledown planted on
    the wind.

And once I met a woman
All in her heart's spring,
But I was a headstrong fool
Heedless of everything,

                              sings Harry.
—I was thistledown planted on the
    wind.

Mustering is the life:
Freed of fears and hopes
I watch the sheep like a pestilence
Pouring over the slopes,

                              sings Harry.
And the past is thistledown planted
    on the wind.

Dream and doubt and the deed
Dissolve like a cloud
On the hills of time.
Be a man never so proud,
                    sings Harry,
He is only thistledown planted on
        the wind.

Themes

What shall we sing? sings Harry.

Sing truthful men? Where shall we find
The man who cares to speak his mind:
Truth's out of uniform, sings Harry,
That's her offence
Where lunacy parades as common sense.

Of lovers then? A sorry myth
To tickle tradesmen's palates with.
Production falls, wise men can prove,
When factory girls dream dreams of love.

Sing of our leaders? Like a pall
Proficiency descends on all
Pontific nobodies who make
Some high pronouncement every week.

Of poets then? How rarely they
Are more than summer shadow-play.
Like canvassers from door to door
The poets go, and gain no ear.

Sing of the fighters? Brave-of-Heart
Soon learns to play the coward's part,
And calls it, breaking solemn pacts,
Fair Compromise or Facing Facts.

Where all around us ancient ills
Devour like blackberry the hills
On every product of the time
Let fall like a poisoned rain of rhyme,
                              sings Harry;
But praise St. Francis feeding crumbs
Into the empty mouths of guns.

What shall we sing? sings Harry.

Sing all things sweet or harsh upon
These islands in the Pacific sun,
The mountains whitened endlessly
And the white horses of the winter sea,
                              sings Harry.

A Woman Shopping

Beauty goes into the butcher's shop
Where blood taints the air;
The chopper comes down on the block
And she pats her hair.

Death's gallery hangs ready
Naked of hair and hide,
But she has clothes on her body
And a heart inside.

What's death to the lady, pray?
Even shopping's a bore.
—The carcasses gently sway
As she goes out the door.

But death goes with her on the way:
In her basket along the street
Rolls heavily against her thigh
The blood-red bud of the meat.

from *Arawata Bill*

The Scene

Mountains nuzzle mountains
White-bearded rock-fronted
In perpetual drizzle.

Rivers swell and twist
Like a torturer's fist
Where the maidenhair
Falls of the waterfall
Sail through the air.

The mountains send below
Their cold tribute of snow
And the birch makes brown
The rivulets running down.

Rock, air, and water meet
Where crags debate
The dividing cloud.

In the dominion of the thorn
The delicate cloud is born,
And golden nuggets bloom
In the womb of the storm.

The Search

What unknown affinity
Lies between mountain and sea
In country crumpled like an unmade bed
Whose crumbs may be nuggets as big as your head
And it's all snow-sheeted, storm-cloud fed?
  Far behind is the blue Pacific,
  And the Tasman somewhere ahead.

Wet or dry, low or high,
Somewhere in a blanketfold of the land
Lies the golden strand.

> Mountain spells may bind it,
> But the marrow in the bone
> The itch in the palm
> The Chinaman's talisman
> To save from harm,
> All tell me I shall find it.

These mountains never stir
In the still or turbulent air.
Only the stones thaw-loosened
Leap from the precipice
Into shrapnel snow-cushioned.

An egg-timer shingle-fan
Dribbles into the pan
And the river sluices with many voices.

> The best pan is an old pan
> —The grains cling to the rust,
> And a few will come from each panning,
> The rust brown, and golden the dust.

But where is the amethyst sky and the high
Mountain of pure gold?

A Prayer

Mother of God, in this brazen sun
Lead me down from the arid heights
Before my strength is done.
Give me the rain
That not long since I cursed in vain.
Lead me to the river, the life-giver.

The River Crossing

The river was announcing
An ominous crossing
With the boulders knocking.

'You can do it and make a fight of it,
Always taking the hard way
For the hell and delight of it.

But there comes the day
When you watch the spate of it,
And camp till the moon's down
—Then find the easy way
Across in the dawn,
Waiting till that swollen vein
Of a river subsides again.'

And Bill set up his camp and watched
His young self, river-cold and scratched,
Struggling across, and up the wrong ridge,
And turning back, temper on edge.

Camp Site

Earth and sky black,
And an old fire's sodden ashes
Were puddled in porridge clay
On that bleak day.

An old coat lay
Like a burst bag, worn
Out in the tussle with thorn.
Water ran
Through a hole in the rusted can.

The pass was wrapped
In a blanket of mist,
And the rain came again,
And the wind whipped.

The climbers had been there camping
Watching the sky
With a weatherwise eye.
And Paradise Pete
Scrabbling a hole in the sleet
When the cloud smote and waters roared
Had scrawled on a piece of board
RIVERS TOO DEEP.

Wata Bill stuck his shovel there
And hung his hat on the handle,
Cutting scrub for a shelter,
Lighting wet wood with a candle.

To The Coast

I

There's no horse this time,
Going's too rough.
It's a man with an eighty-pound pack,
And that's more than enough.

> *Always the colour, in quartz or the river,*
> *Never the nuggets as large as a liver.*

Five years ago I tried this route
Taking the left branch. Now try the right.
It'll mean tramping half the night
Before the weather breaks, turning
Tarns into lakes.

The colour is elusive, like streaks
Of wind-cloud. Gold dust must
Come from somewhere. But where?

Neither river nor mountain speaks.

III

Jacksons Bay on the Tasman, the end
Of many a search round many a bend.

Does the terminus of the sea
Contain my mystery,
Throwing back on the beach
Grains of gold
I have followed from sea to sea
Thirty times and again
Since I was thirty years old?

A seaboot full of gold, tempest tossed,
They hid somewhere on the coast
When their ship was lost.

But back to the mountains!
I know
The fire of gold
Lies under that cold snow.

Soliloquies

III

When God made this place
He made mountains and fissures
Hostile, vicious, and turned
Away His face.

Did He mean me to burn out my heart
In a forty-year search
In this wilderness
Of snow and black birch,
With only a horse for company
Beating on a white tympany?

Is this some penance
For a sin I never knew,
Or does my grail
Still lie in the snow or hail?

Yet it might be His purpose to plant
The immaculate metal
Where the stoutest hearts quail.

IV

They'll not laugh this time
When I come home
With something in my poke.
They've been saying too long
That Arawata Bill's just a joke.

The fools! There's more gold beneath
These rivers and mountains
Than in all their clattering teeth.

The Crystallized Waves

Snow is frozen cloud
Tumbled to the ravine,
The mist and the mountain-top
Lying between.

The cloud turns to snow or mist,
The mist to the stream,
The stream seeks out the ocean
All in a geographer's dream.

What are the mountains on high
But the crystallized waves of the sea,
And what is the white-topped wave
But a mountain that liquidly weaves?

The water belongs to the mountain,
Belongs to the deep;
The mountain beneath the water
Suckles oceans in sleep.

How are the tops in the dawn?

The End

It got you at last, Bill,
The razor-edge that cut you down
Not in the gullies nor on the pass
But in a bed in town.

R.I.P. where no gold lies
But in your own questing soul
Rich in faith and a wild surmise.

You should have been told
Only in you was the gold:
Mountain and river paid you no fee,
Mountain melting to the river,
River to the sea.

PAUL HENDERSON

Object Lesson

A hill you may say is a hill; take a hill,
Or a group of them forming an island,
Range, or peninsula. Here's the benign
Slope, thrust of deceptive hand
Green-gloved over the strong racked bones
Of earth assaulting sky. Follow the up,
The flow, the final burst in the sun;
Measure the cone; a hill, you perceive, is a hill.
A man you may say is a man; but when
He's extended himself to the hill, included
The spur and the curve in the light of his
Knowing how this was formed; pondered if
Time, place, thought and strewn heaven
Matter a tinker's curse; noticed the blue
Haze hills absorb from the sea, clouds
Cumbering the island; known the slight
Fear of far hills, and the sweet solace
Of these, being home; then we consider again
Well, what is a hill? Is it a hill,
Or a hill through the eyes of one human?

Return Journey

Wellington again slaps the face with wind
So well remembered; and now the mind
Leaps; all sea, all tossed hills, all white-
Edged air poured in tides over the tight
Town. Bleached bones of houses are hard
To distinguish, at some distance, from a graveyard.

145

But do not consider death; we have tucked
Too snugly into the valleys; we have mucked
With the rake of time over the tamed
Foreshore. Battering trams; Lambton, lamed
With concrete, has only a hint of ghost waters
On the Quay stranded among elevators.

There is no need to remember swamp-grass,
Or how the first women (let the rain pass,
They had prayed) wept when the hills reared up
Through the mist, and they were trapped
Between sea and cliffed forest. No ship could be
More prisoning than the grey beach at Petone.

No need to consider (here where we have shut
The tiger tight behind iron and concrete)
How we might yet drown deep under the wind;
And the wind die too; and an insect find
(Columbus of his day) the little graveyard town
Set in a still landscape like porcelain.

Elegy

I

Morning after death on the bar was calm;
There was no difficulty in looking for the boy's body.
The boat had been found in the dark, overturned,
And at dawn the men went out again
To search the beaches and sweep, in the boats, offshore.
The mountains to the north stood up like sepulchres
Rising white-boned out of a black sea.
The flat hymnal of light lay asleep in the sky
And sang morning in a minor key
To wake the wheeling flights of birds
That, curious, mark down all drifting wrack
And disabled drowned bodies.

He should not have attempted the bar, of course;
The tide was ebbing but he was making for home.
On the wide sea with night falling,
Only the open, small yacht to uplift him,
He must have felt, well, try it.

Moments make miniature green globes in the mind;
Light flaring on dark from house windows
As the lifeboat slid out on the ways;
Searchlight like an awed moon at sea
Probing the black night and white breakers,
A drawn will of the anxious, twining a tight knot
In the shadows of Shag Rock; car lights
A stereoscopic, too brutal revelation of tears.

The shocked boy saying that his friend was gone;
That they'd found the boat, turned turtle,
But that Jack was lost, they couldn't find him.

O weep all night for this drowned youth,
Waiting in the rock's black arms for the foreseen time
Of lifeboat returning, lonely, in the small hours;
Of certainty frozen in the immutable shape of hands;
Of a boy's boat is no bond, nor even a safe coffin.

Get some sleep, if you can; by now he's dead,
The water is too cold, it is almost winter.

3

Yet at dawn they were searching the beaches.
In the immense dawn distances the groups of men
Walked like little pins over the sandspits
And the morning light broke bitterly like snowflakes

147

On the sun-dazed self-conscious sea
That tight-lipped along the beaches hides
Its dreadful truths, its doused, its double-drowned boys
Lying like Jonahs in a beast's belly.

The sun rose on a silver-lidded sea that lapped
Over the sandbanks like turning shillings,
Making enormous shadows which, when reached,
Were nothing at all. In such confusion
Of light and lazing sand-pipers and lumps of seaweed
How find in this vast soul of silver and of sand
All that is left of one boy?

Yet at noon the beast opened its lips,
Or perhaps it was just that, with the sun higher,
The light was no longer tricky, but anyway
The boy was spewed up, and the body was seen
Floating face down, in a life-jacket, beyond the surf.

So is the sea-god fed, and one more sacrifice
Strewn on the waves. No fairer limbs
Are demanded, their separate toll will delay
Disaster in the mind's millennial time and kiss
The countless bare noons where there are no shadows.

It was easy enough then to go out on surf-skis,
Into the light that by afternoon would be blue,
And bring in the boy's body, for a calmer burial.

I Think of Those

Sometimes I think of those whose lives touch mine
Too briefly; who, by a look or word, show me
A little of what lies beneath, but, leaving then,
Because we are trained to silence, they are shut away.

How shall I tell one friend from casual passer
Who am walled also in self; and cannot say
Do not hesitate; here is a love without fear;
The mind in its lonely prison forfeits today

As well as its yesterdays; and black tomorrows
Are chained with the hooded falcon on time's wrist
Unknowing and therefore unenvious of ecstatic arrow
Flight when the dark bird is released.

Yet I come to you in these words as surely
As though you were here surprised again at my eyes,
Though if this be all, if there is never any
If there is never between us more, no such awakening dies.

M. K. JOSEPH

Off Cape Leeuwen

Leviathan the ocean, spiked and mailed,
Scalloped with imbricated scales,
With clots of granite clawed and tailed
(His parasites are wandering whales)

Hails in Behemoth the ship
A creature of the self-same mould
Nonchalantly in iron grip
Bearing its passengers embowelled.

Leviathan's somnolent shoulder nudges
Behemoth's ridged and riveted flank,
Who majestically heaving, sideways budges
Flounders and skids like a mudded tank,

Poises straddling, wavers and heels,
Peers at the moon with squinted face,
Then hip and shoulder to Leviathan reels
In a solemn brotherly drunken embrace.

Above them in sky's spinning dome
Stars bloom to meteors at each roll—
These tipsy monsters reeling home
Between Australia and the Pole.

Nurse's Song

It's better not to ask, not to deny
But soothe the baby with a lullaby
Nor hint his legacy of grace and grief
Of state and sorrow, bearing and belief.

The palace duties and the palace joys;
The Dauphin howling at his emerald toys
The Infanta in a grape-skin velvet dressed
Low cut to show the glamour of her breast;

The ebony and ivory of the table
In circled candle-light; the hand scarce able
To lift the monstrous amethyst, which afar
Shines to its trembling like a dancing star;

The polished galleries on a summer night
Ablaze like rivers in the thunderous light
(Still and unwinking stood the halberdiers
As the cloaked figure passed with sound of tears);

The chapel where, by chantry screen, there sings
A youth leading responses to the king's
Obsequies, whose lineaments he bore.
He sings in sweet soprano evermore.

Distilled Water

From Blenheim's clocktower a cheerful bell bangs out
The hour, and time hangs humming in the wind.
Time and the honoured dead. What else? The odd
Remote and shabby peace of a provincial town.
Blenkinsopp's gun? the Wairau massacre?
Squabbles in a remote part of empire.
Some history. Some history, but not much.

Consider now the nature of distilled
Water which has boiled and left behind
In the retort rewarding sediment
Of salts and toxins. Chemically pure of course
(No foreign bodies here) but to the taste
Tasteless and flat. Let it spill on the ground,

Leach out its salts, accumulate its algae,
Be living: the savour's in impurity.
Is that what we are? something that boiled away
In the steaming flask of nineteenth-century Europe?
Innocuous until now, or just beginning
To make its own impression on the tongue.

And through the Tory Channel naked hills
Gully and slip pass by, monotonously dramatic
Like bad blank verse, till one cries out for
Enjambement, equivalence, modulation,
The studied accent of the human voice,
Or the passage opening through the windy headlands
Where the snowed Kaikouras hang in the air like mirage
And the nation of gulls assembles on the waters
Of the salt sea that walks about the world.

Mercury Bay Eclogue

Dominus regnavit, exsultet terra: laetentur insulae multae.

I

The child's castle crumbles; hot air shimmers
Like water working over empty sand.
Summer noon is long and the brown swimmers
For fear of outward currents, lie on land.
With tumbleweed and seashells in its hand
The wind walks, a vigorous noonday ghost
Bearing gifts for an expected guest.

Hull down on horizon, island and yacht
Vanish into blue leaving no trace;
Above my head the nebulae retreat
Dizzily sliding round the bend of space
Winking a last red signal of distress.
Each galaxy or archipelago
Plunges away into the sky or sea.

In the dry noon are all things whirling away?
They are whirling away, but look—the gull's flight,
Stonefall towards the rainbows of the spray
Skim swim and glide on wing up to the light
And in this airy gesture of delight
See wind and sky transformed to bless and warn,
The dance, the transfiguration, the return.

The turning wheels swing the star to harbour
And rock the homing yacht in a deep lull,
Bring children to their tea beneath the arbour,
Domesticate the wind's ghost and pull
Islands to anchor, softly drop the gull
Into his nest of burnished stones and lead
The yachtsmen and the swimmers to their bed.

II

A shepherd on a bicycle
Breaks the pose of pastoral
   But will suffice to keep
   The innocence of sheep.

Ringing his bell he drives the flock
From sleepy field and wind-scarred rock
   To where the creaming seas
   Wash shoreward like a fleece.

The farmer and his wife emerge
All golden from the ocean-surge
   Their limbs and children speak
   The legend of the Greek.

The shadowy tents beneath the pines
The surfboards and the fishing-lines
   Tell that our life might be
   One of simplicity.

The wind strums aeolian lyres
Inshore among the telephone wires
   Linking each to each.
   The city and the beach.

For sunburnt sleepers would not come
If inland factories did not hum
   And this Arcadian state
   Is built on butterfat.

So children burn the seastained wood
And tell the present as a good
   Knowing that bonfires are
   Important as a star.

And on his gibbet the swordfish raised
With bloody beak and eye glazed
   Glares down into the tide
   Astonishment and pride.

Machine once muscled with delight
He merges now in primitive night;
   The mild and wondering crowd
   Admire the dying god
   Where Kupe and where Cook have trod.

III

Over the sea lie Europe and Asia
   The dead moulded in snow
The persecution of nuns and intellectuals
   The clever and the gentle
The political trials and punishment camps
   The perversion of children
Men withering away with fear of the end.

Fifteen years of a bad conscience
  Over Spain and Poland
Vienna Berlin Israel Korea
  Orphans and prostitutes
Unburied the dead and homeless living
  We looked on ruined cities
Saying, These are our people.

We sat in the sun enduring good luck
  Like the stain of original sin
Trying to be as God, to shoulder
  The world's great sorrow
Too shaken to see that we hadn't the talent
  That the clenching heart is a fist
And a man's grasp the reach of his arm.

Be still and know: the passionate intellect
  Prepares great labours
Building of bridges, practice of medicine.
  Still there are cows to be milked
Students to teach, traffic direction
  Ships unloading at wharves
And the composition of symphonies.

IV

The poets standing on the shelf
Excavate the buried self
Freud's injunction they obey
Where id was, let ego be.

Yeats who from his tower sees
The interlocking vortices
Of the present and the past,
Shall find the centre hold at last.

Eliot whose early taste
Was for the cenobitic waste
Now finds the promise of a pardon
Through children's laughter in the locked garden.

Pound in his barbed-wire cage
Prodded into stuttering rage
Still earns reverence from each
Because he purified our speech.

Cavalier or toreador
Is Campbell expert to explore
The truthful moment when we face
The black bull in the arid place.

And Auden who has seen too much
Of the wound weeping for the healer's touch
A surgeon in his rubber gloves
Now cauterizes where he loves.

The summer landscape understood
The morning news, the poet's mood,
By their imperatives are defined
Converging patterns in the mind.

V

Come fleet Mercury, messenger of gods and men
Skim with your winged sandal the resounding surf
Quickly come bearing to all things human
Celestial medicine for their tongueless grief.
Heaven's thief and merchant, here is your port
Lave with your gifts of healing and of speech
All mortals who shall ever print with foot
These silent hills and this forsaken beach.

Come sweet Venus, mother of men and beasts
While meteors fall across the yellow moon
Above the hills herded like sleeping beasts,
Sweetly come lady, and with hand serene
Plant fruits of peace where by this mariner's mark
The torrents of your sea-begetting roar
And trouble in their dreams of glowing dark
These sleeping hills and this forbidden shore.

Come swift ship and welcome navigators
Link and line with your instruments this earth
To heaven under the propitious stars,
Show forth the joined and fortune-bearing birth
And set this fallen stone a meteorite
Where Mercury and Venus hand in hand
Walk on the waters this auspicious night
And touch to swift love this forgotten strand.

Girl, Boy, Flower, Bicycle

This girl
Waits at the corner for
This boy
Freewheeling on his bicycle.
She holds
A flower in her hand
A gold flower
In her hands she holds
The sun.
With power between his thighs
The boy
Comes smiling to her
He rides
A bicycle that glitters like
The wind.

This boy this girl
They walk
In step with the wind
Arm in arm
They climb the level street
To where
Laid on the glittering handlebars
The flower
Is round and shining as
The sun.

GLORIA RAWLINSON

The Islands Where I was Born

I

Fragrances that like a wind disturb
The child's pacific dry in suburban shell
And send it murmuring through time's bony curb
Have caught me in the glassbright thoroughfare:
Pineapples oranges limes, their island smell
A catspaw rocking heart to hoist and dare
The long remembrance. Heart, if you would mime
Journeys to where a child blinked half the truth
Let points of origin be fixed where time
May be measured for a meaningful azimuth;
Your flowery isles are masked in Medusa's blood
And the sapphiry elements wear a darker hood.

II

There was no Pacific then, reef-broken spray
Flared on extremities of childish vision,
Under the mango tree's dim acre, at play
In sunflower groves I lived my changeless season.

When insular hours with morning steps unfurled
Chickens and coconuts, bronze fisherboy,
And old deaf Ka Ngutu's wagon howled
Past the tree of flying foxes it seemed that joy

Was born like my shadow in the sun's presence
With fuming orange in hand and the everywhere
Odour steaming from copra's oily crescents
Soothed and smoothed the least rebellious air.

Then foster speech of my Friendly Islands tongue
Could wag its music, the Ofa Atu sworn
With a white smile and all sweet change sung
For trade or gift or guile where I was born.

And I didn't believe in that realm of banished fairies
The Graveyard of Disobedient Children and hushed
Sleepers who once ran hatless, ate tapu'd berries
Or cut their feet on coral and never confessed.

For then I thought we lived on the only route,
In the apple of a heavenly eye, the fond
Providence of flowery oils and fruit,
Kingdom of Joy and Enjoy to the farthest frond.

It was out of all reckoning one last Steamer Day
When I saw the Pacific skyward beyond our coral;
Farewells fluttered . . . palm-trees turned away
And cool on my cheeks the wind from a new littoral.

III

The key was your clear maternal voice
In stories drolled like a deepsea shell
Except they smacked of human salt
And fancy that your witty mind
Spun from the long-fetched tale,
But colour was counted less than fault
Since truth was nearest to be found
In the swift light of your humorous eyes.

Friends at our fireside listened and laughed.
I blazed with private wonder.
You spoke of places I knew when small
But Oh how far may living stretch?
How many fathoms does heart fall under?
And mind grows—how many mountains tall?
The world's wild wisdom sang out of reach
Till one had learned its tortuous craft.

IV

They were our legends, we flagged them on our lives;
Though tattered with telling I wouldn't haul them down!
Sometimes you remembered the two days' journey
'—in a boat rigged with twine, leaking at every seam.
When a tall sea rushed upon us
Thrust the roaring tongue-tip of its swell
Under the boozing timbers, how they groaned, staggered
    down!
One small rusty tin was our bailer
And this I scooped in the settling weight of our death
While the Tongan crew prayed and sang for mercy of our
    lives.
And how we survived, by craft or prayer or bailer
Seems crazy now, and the last thing to be dreamed
That land's relief humped on the reddening west.'
    'Jiali was the girl from Nukualofa
Swam forty miles from where a boat went down.
Through the sun-beaten, shark-schooled waters
Armed with a high heart swam the long day home;
When, her hair snatched on coral, the foaming breakers
Shelved her torn and screaming on the reef,
    She said a spirit wouldn't let her drown.'
'Hunting one brilliant midnight by calm lagoon
And burning copra to range the wild pigs near,
No grunting, no scuffle we heard, no sound
But where our horses pulled on their tethered reins
And the inward step by step of mounting fear.
Then smashing mirrored light with gulching waves
Lunged to the shoregrass out of the lagoon
A huge sea-beast, ball-eyed, long-necked, frill-maned.
Leaping to horse we saw with twisted glance
That image, unforgettable, reared at the moon.'
    'Once on an island voyage
A mating of whales, the thing most rarely seen;
How she, pale belly up, lay still on the moving blue,

And was the centre of the circling bull;
How whorling out to the rim of the sky he turned
And shirring a leaguelong wake flashed for his centre.
And they at the clash stood up like two enormous columns,
Fell with splashing thunder, rolled over and under,
Down through the sealight's fathoms, into the ocean's
　　　night.'
　　　　　'Eua Iki! Quite lacking in mementoes
And I never thought to bring back seeds and cuttings.
Rips, foam-fierce, guarded the narrow entry,
Bucking between the reefs you were cannoned ashore.
They were silks of sand one stepped on, warm and shining
As the island's phantasy. No one would believe . . .
Flowers, but I can't name them,
Stemmed perhaps from that oldest and richest of gardens.
　　　　　We skipped on ropes of orchids
In moist rock-hollows hung with trumpeting vines;
　　　　　Roamed little valleys
Where grass like green mice meadowed tiny ponies;
　　　　　Bathed in crystal—
Clear sweet fathoms, watching jewels of fish in the coral-
　　　trees—
(They matched I thought the giant butterflies in the sun's
　　　gleam.)
　　　　　Slept at last to the island's
Soft Ariel untragic sigh of a futureless dream.
Sometimes I wonder was it really so.'
Years later you remembered
'Eua Iki lies on the edge of the Tongan Deep.'

V

The stars that sing for recollective sails
With no iron pulling at the point of pleasure
Are child and dreamer exulting in fabled isles
That Maui fished out of the dolphined azure.

'The goldless age where gold disturbs no dreams',
So Byron burning for a south could sigh
With lovesweet oil of his romantic themes
Drawn from the leaves of Mariner and Bligh.

Perhaps that goldless age is the fruit-full sense
Of the islands where I was born, when servitor
Of earthly wishes the sun spreads an immense
Glitter over the Deep's unfathomable sore.

The Tongan Deep! Like death's gut or time's cleft
One grinding yard for dug-out galleon schooner,
Husking bones and bells to pelagic drift,
Repelling our brightest reason, the quick lunar

Tides of our laughter and grief with a quietest mouth.
Thereover we blue-weather-wise would sail
Leaving the wounded day unturned for truth
But mind hears soundings, haulnets a dragon's scale

And must pursue beyond the serving sun
Its utter depth; as Oh, wild-fire-west hurled
To the cod of the track its vast hurricane
Of gilded dreams across the nescient world.

But old as man the island ghosts that rise
From sacrificial stones, purgations of history,
Rinse with undying rains our turnaway eyes
Till the coiled mountain sombres the sapphire sea.

Fear we to know these things? The changing wind
Itself must halt before the Royal Tombs,
Old Lord Tortoise wanders battered and blind
Who shielded his sleep against a thousand dooms;

So in the metropolis panged by the day's alarms
Sail for that strength of witness you recall
By heart to the Friendly Kingdom, its crooked palms
Shall say what pacific hands environ all.

VI

Who is the dancer
Sways at her anchorage
By the salt grave?
The palmtree our sister
Of Adam's red clay;
Slantset by hurricane
Stripped to bone courage
She claps like a scaredevil
Through the moon's and sun's day.

Who are the singers
With timebeat and palmclap
Shake the green grave?
Brown lass, brown lad,
Of sweet banqueting heart:
Earth's night is long
But laughing they clip
Hibiscus and jasmine
In their hair, in their song.

Merry-go-round

All day where Megaphone
the gala tyrant booms
twelve painted animals
wind up the clockwise dreams

of mounted cherubs with
brave eyes and comet curls,
while groundlings wait their turn
scuffing impatient heels.

Whirled like a stars' cavalcade
they spin on a glittering core,
pumped by the hot serenade
their young blood could pirouette for—
ever and ever and ever and ever

O children ride the swan,
ride the zebra, ride
the only tiger you
are really safe upon.

For time will halt the rounds,
silence and moonlight share
your popcorn bags, your cones,
and grinning melonrinds.

The Hare in the Snow

Afraid and trackless between storm and storm
Runs the mountain hare blinded with snow,
Digs in its dazzle her last desperate form
But seeks a refuge not a death below.

What shall our utmost clarity unlock?

Where she had rooted for her darkened hope
Time, immense, unhumbled, turns with the sun
Stripping snows down to adamantine rock:
All that's left of grief on the bright slope
Discover now—a small crouched skeleton.

RUTH DALLAS

Deserted Beach

If there had been one bird, if there had been
One gull to circle through the wild salt wind
Or cry above the breaking of the waves,
One footprint or one feather on the sand,
Then the great rocks leaning from the hills
Might have been the ruins of great walls.

Because no bird flew there, because there was
Nothing on that beach that called or sang,
The rocks leaned out towards the sea and watched
As women watch beside the sea day-long,
Shut within themselves like flowers in rain,
For men and ships that will not come again.

Of that warm moment when they rang with song,
Threw back the clink of sharpened stone on stone,
When firelight dimmed the stars, and when they heard
Above the lonely sea-sound, creak and groan
Of keels on shingle, nothing now remained
But oven-stones, and mounds of shells and sand.

If there had been one bird—but no; as once
For pillar, pyramid, and lion, all
Rock waited, still the great rocks waited, watched;
No cry of child or gull above the fall
Of waves on stones. Only the sea moved there,
And weeds within the waves like floating hair.

Grandmother and Child

The waves that danced about the rock have gone,
The tide has stolen the rock as time has stolen
The quiet old lady who waited beneath the trees
That moved with a sad sea-sound in the summer wind.

When death was as near as the wind among the leaves,
Troubling the waking fear in the heart of the child
As the wind was troubling the shadows on the sunlit lawn,
The grandmother seemed as frail as the frailest leaf.

But she sat so still in the shade of the summer trees
With the wind of death on her cheeks and her folded hands,
Her strength seemed large and cool, as the rock in the sea
Seemed large and cool in the green and restless waves.

As the rock remains in the sea, deep down and strong,
The rock-like strength of the lady beneath the trees
Remains in the mind of the child, more real than death,
To challenge the child's strength in the hour of fear.

A Striped Shell

Not for us this shell grew like a lily,
Is striped outside and ivory within,
Too many flower-like shells have been washed up
And crushed and scattered on these wild beaches,
Spin and glint along the blowing sand.

A shell must have some shape, but you would think
That any shape would serve, any colour;
And then the way they break through all that seems
Dark and threatening in the sea, as strangely
Easily as snowdrops through dead leaves.

167

It is the same with every beautiful thing
Perhaps that breaks through darkness or decay,
But here where we walk warily, at times
In places where no man has been before,
These things are startling held against the silence.

If it is not a striped and rounded shell
Found unharmed among sharp rocks or under
Yellow snakes of weed, it is a fern
That seems too delicate to touch uncurling
In the gloom of some deep forest glade.

Behind a shell that fills and cups the hand,
Ferns that shine like sunlight through dark trees,
Must lie innumerable shells and ferns
No man has seen, shells like this, and ferns
As delicate as any we have found.

If only one could learn to accept this shell
For what it is; but there is something in
Its shape and colour, something in its breaking
Like a flower from the sea, that makes one
Turn it over in the hand, and over.

The Boy

Miraculously in the autumn twilight, out of
The wet-grass smell of the apple, out of the cold
Smooth feel of it against his shrunken fingers,
He made the boy; he was not there before,
A boy in the trailing apple branches hiding,
Surprising us like the cobwebs hung with rain
That suddenly shone from the darkness under the leaves.

Out of the apple he made the boy, the apple
So pensively turned and turned in the rainy twilight,
Cold yellow apple out of his childhood heavy
Again in his hand. So quietly he stood,
Under dark leaves, shoulders and grey head bent,
Cupped fingers gnarled and knotty as old twigs,
He seemed at first another apple tree.

Then he made the boy, the boy who still
In autumn twilight shakes, when no wind stirs,
The yellow apples from the trees, or swings
On the oldest boughs; but he was not the boy;
We could in a moment see the tight-skinned apple
Fall and open into roots and leaves,
But never the hands grow into the boy's young hands.

A Tea-shop

If in the scent of violets there came
The moment only, then how warm the spring
And even the little flower-shops would seem
With their forced winter blooms; but violets bring
A rush of uninvited details, two
Great tattered leaves, deep wrinkled and dull green,
That almost hide the tiny flowers, blue
As far-off hills before the fall of rain;
They bring the grey light in the tea-shop, sound
Of people in the street, their wooden-heeled
Quick stepping through the chill September wind;
And clear as the cups of tea that have grown cold,
    The face of an old sad woman sitting near,
    Side on, with a large bright ear-ring in her ear.

from *Letter to a Chinese Poet*

Beating the Drum

Warming a set of new bones
In the old fire of the sun, in the fashion
Of all men, and lions, and blackbirds,
Finding myself upon the planet earth,
Abroad on a short journey
Equipped with heart and lungs to last
Not as long as a house, or a peony rose,
Travelling in the midst of a multitude
Of soft and breathing creatures
In skins of various colours, feathers, fur,
A tender population
For a hard ball spinning
Indifferently through light and dark,
I turn to an old poem,
Fresh as this morning's rose,
Though a thousand summers have shed their blooms
Since the bones that guided brush or pen
Were dust upon the wind.

So men turned to a carved stick
That held the lonely history of the tribe.

Round the sun and round the sun and round.

We have left the tree and waterhole
For a wilderness of stars.

Round the sun and round the sun and round.

I sing the carvers of sticks and the makers of poems,
This man who worked on ivory,
That one who shaped a fine jar,
And the man who painted a cave wall
By the light of fire.

Reminded in the noon hour
With the sun warm upon the bone
Under the canopy of the climbing rose,
That man is cut down like a flower,
I sing the makers
Of all things true and fair that stand
When the wind has parted
The warm and obedient bones of the hand;
All those I sing,
And among them name your name,
Who left the earth richer than when they came.

The rose is shaken in the wind,
Round the sun
The petals fall
And round the sun and round.

Among Old Houses

In every second back yard
Maimed and rheumaticky branches swell
And break
                violently
Into shell-clear petals calm as porcelain,

Or foam afloat behind a travelling wave.

No yard made hideous by discarded oil-drums,
Rusted scrap-iron, crates, collapsing sheds,
That is not visited by madcap Spring;
It's not just one old tree that glitters forth,
Not two, but tree on blossoming tree—
A fairytale procession, like the arrival
Of twenty sisters ready for a ball,
Or mermaids, voluptuous, glistening from the sea.

Over the pates of the old men thawing
Their cold limbs in the spring sun,
Over the leaping children, over wheels
Still bound and netted with last year's straws,
On angel and sinner, on all, on all,
                                        like rice,
Like a gift, like a blessing,
            The immaculate petals fall.

Shadow Show

Watch, now.
From this black paper,
If I cut a silhouette,
Hands blown sideways by unceasing winds,
Shoulders bowed under a burden,
Knees bent,
A birdsclaw foothold on the earth,
You could say that I made a tree,
Storm twisted.

Or a woman, or a man.

HUBERT WITHEFORD

Elegy in the Orongorongo Valley

Sundered from this beauty is its fond lover
Who wandered in boredom over far oceans
Again and again remembering, till the day
When decks split in flame and the sea choked him.

Did his despairing salt-water stormed eye-balls
Search, as they broke, for these streams sprawling
Over high places, the mountains of springtime,
Out of the world on a lost morning?

Did death's lightning show him this shadowed valley
Burning through oceans, green beyond time?
Was this the river he felt closing over
Islands of pain and over his life?

Here and in exile and in last anguish
He found no frenzy to win him this wanton—
In his full failure glistens the wild bush
Too long remembered, too long forgotten.

The Waters, Indeed, are to the Palate, Bitter

Half my life has passed me by
In my island washed around
By desert seas and void security—
Each year my heart becomes more dry.

Through nerveless fingers life like rice
In slow storm runs to the ground;
Not distance nor insentience provides
Cuirass against that mild fatality.

173

And slowly, slowly, our life flows
To the proud blaring of the Tramways Band
By postered walls of corrugated iron
And past abominable bungalows.

Slow though that blast, its taste of failure stings
As the salt spray from out the seething waste
Scalds, on the naked headland, human lips.
Let me fathom that sheer taste.

The Cactuses

It is the orange flower on dark-flushed stem
Or the small spines to guard the so sleek flesh,
Amid dry sand and stone,
That waken an almost malicious love
For the mild cunning of the old creation.
Unblurred by virtue's or by sin's delusion
Out of the inert debris of disaster
It rose among the thinning atmosphere.
We cannot emulate. But, as across the aeons
Our later sense accosts these presences,
A sting of freshness runs from skull to heel
And, on the palate, sparkling waters fleet.

At the Discharge of Cannon Rise the Drowned

One forfeit more from life the current claimed
While, on the horizon, rose white-sheeted spars;
Bare of their canvas when the morning came
They rode the bay that held its prisoner.

Some days then, by our time, of windless rain
That poured and ebbed to shroud or almost show
The unpeopled decks, the looming guardian
On the phantasmal world where no clock marks
Duration of the cold abandonments
And weird acceptances that lead man hence.

Till from the flickering scene one stark vignette
Glares in ambiguous hues of hope and death—
Out of a port-hole bursts a smear of flame,
A blast of thunder from the flood rebounds.
With gliding leap, impelled by answering fire,
Lazarus rises from his restless couch.

Now his corrupted life is as the charge
Exploded in the cannon's narrow depth.
Native no longer of the earth, he springs,
Breaking the waters he surrendered in
And, as he leaves the limbo of vague dream,
Out of the wash and weed he plucks his death.

Back, then, from harbour to the mounting storm,
Into the gale that blows from their high port,
Back from mortality the vast sails slide.

King of Kings

The Emperor (you've heard?) went by this road.
Ahead, police, postillions, cuirassiers;
Behind, ambassadors, air-marshals, equerries,
And, all around, this mild, unjubilant crowd.
I saw the Emperor?
Well, no. It seemed important to be there.
I'd travelled far. Spent my life's savings, too.
But, while I looked at the half-witted horsemens' plumes
And thought of some of what was wrong with me,
I saw his back, receding down new streets.

Snow

You like those images of snow that ask emotion,
Or press their chromium blade against the skin
Or trick the little surface of the brain.

You do not want
The dazzling, *naïf*, still descending one.

Cloud Burst

The fuchsia and I seem happy now.
Up from the sun-hard soil the rain is bouncing
And lightning bursts out of the afternoon.
The radio
Crackles with anger much more lively than the dim
Threats of peace-loving statesmen that it drowns.
Closer
Reverberations. Flower-pots overflow.
Even the heart
Has burst its calyx of anxieties;
The spouting
Cascades superbly into two brown shoes
Put carefully—by someone else—out in the yard.
The lightning makes a difference to the room.

The Displacement

How can I look at my unhappiness
As it puts its hand over the side
Of the crumbling old well
And hooks itself up?
I know without opening my eyes
It is ugly,
It is mine.

It is really not unhappiness at all,
Who is to tell what it is?
It is something pressing up toward the light;
I call it ugly but feel only it is obscene,
A native, perhaps beautiful, of the vasty deep.

Barbarossa

Addiction to the exceptional event—
That flaw
In something like *My Childhood Days in X*,
And fault-line—as from the Aleutians
Down the Pacific to where I was when
It opened wide one day when I was ten.

The town-hall whistle blows. It's five
To twelve. Now homewards, slow,
Turning a legend like a stone, sea-worn,
Red-streaked. The bearded Emperor in the German cave
Sits in his armour; when will he wake and go
Clanking into the light to lead his hordes?

The gutters heave.
          Upon the rumbling ground
I balance. I sit down.
A stop to stories of the death of kings.
I watch the telegraph
Poles. A great hand plucks the strings.

Upon the other coast Napier, too, sways
Most irrecoverably: flames. Looters are shot
By landing-parties near the gutted shops.
Half a hill
Spilt on the coast-road; squashed in their ancient Fords
The burghers sit there still.

Bondage

Watching the lightning
On the Basin d'Arcachon
Link the sea to the sky,
Atlantic with Gironde,

I sit, and there might be
Just the cold glass in my hand,
Far storm, the tropic breeze,
The *plage*—neon-lit, abandoned.

But flashing in my skull
I feel that other chain
From cell to clattering cell
Saying

'You have been here too long' and 'Go
Back. Tell her to come.'
Blaze, forked conjunctions,
Who dares to stand alone?

The Arena

The life drains out. In drops and spurts it flows
And, as it runs, I move. In stops and goes.
Lurching, spasmodic, I draw nearer to
The obscure centre I have turned around,
My forty years—say 'God', say 'sex',
But know the sensual bound
While strength leaks
Out, of life within, the race against the wheel
Spun faster every month, each month more fell.

A wound takes time and resurrection more.
Slowly I cross this room,
What will have died before I reach a door?

White Goddess

When will she come again—

The milk-white muse,
Whose wings, spread sheer, close in
Over the nightmare and the activeness?
'Like any living orgasm'
As the man stranded there,
At the bright-bottled bar,
Anxiously says of his roses.

They, too, are in question.

KEITH SINCLAIR

Memorial to a Missionary

*Thomas Kendall, 1778–1832, first resident missionary in
New Zealand, author of* The New Zealanders' First Book
(1815), grandfather of the Australian poet, H. C. Kendall.

Instructed to speak of God with emphasis
On sin and its consequence, to cannibals
Of the evil of sin, he came from father's farm,
The virtuous home, the comfortable chapel,
The village school, so inadequately armed,
His mail of morals tested in drawing-rooms,
Not war, to teach his obscure and pitied pupils.

There were cheers in Clapham, prayers in Lincolnshire,
Psalms on the beaches, praise, O hope above.
Angels sang as he built the south's first school,
For Augustine had landed with the love
Of God at the Bay; he would speak for his aims were full
Of Cranmer, Calvin; would teach for he brought the world
Of wisdom, dreamed of the countless souls to save.

But though he cried with a voice of bells none heard,
For who was to find salvation in the sounds
Of English words? The scurrilous sailors spoke
More clearly with rum and lusting, so he turned
To the native vowels for symbols, sought to make
The Word of God anew, in the tribes' first book
Laying in Christ's advance a path of nouns.

Seeking the Maori name for sin, for hell,
Teacher turned scholar he sat at Hongi's feet
And guns were the coin he paid for revelation.
To the south men died when Hongi spent his fees.

Wrestling with meanings that defied translation,
Christian in seeking truth found sorcery,
Pilgrim encountered sex in philosophy.

A dreaming hour he spent at that mast of a tree,
And apple of his eye his mother withheld was that love,
The night of feeling, was pure and mooned for man,
Woman was made of earth and earth for wife.
In following their minds he found the men
And reached for a vision past his mother-land,
Converted by heathen he had come to save.

He drank the waters of the underworld
Lying all day in the unconverted flesh,
Entangled in old time, before Christ's birth,
Beyond redemption, found what a nest of bliss,
A hot and mushroom love lay fair in the fern
To suck from his soul the lineaments of desire,
And leave despair, O damned undreamed of pleasures.

To cure the sick at soul the little doctor
Sought out an ardent tonic far too hot,
Though not forbidden, for his infirmity.
With the south on his tongue and sweet he had forgotten
His mission, thirsted for infinities
Of the secret cider and its thick voice in the throat,
Bringing the sun all a-blossom to his blood.

But as sudden and in between such dawns his conscience
Sharpened his sins to prick his heart like nails.
The hell the Christian fears to name was heaven
To his fierce remorse and heaven and hell
Were the day and night in his life and wasted him
With their swift circling passions, until he cursed
In prayers but hated the flush of his concupiscence.

Did he fall through pride of spirit, through arrogance
Or through humility, not scorning the prayers
Of savages and their intricate pantheon?
He lacked the confident pity of his brethren.
To understand he had to sympathize,
Then felt, and feeling, fell, one man a breath
In the human gale of a culture's thousand years.

The unfaithful shepherd was sent from the farm of souls
To live, a disgraceful name in the Christian's ear,
A breathing sin among the more tolerant chiefs.
An outcaste there, or preaching where he fled
To Valparaiso from devils and reproof,
Or coasting logs round Sydney, still he strove
To find the life in the words his past had said.

Drowning off Jervis Bay, O the pain,
For death is a virgin rich in maidenheads
And memories, trees two hundred feet and tall.
The sea is a savage maiden, in her legs
Sharp pangs no missionary drank before,
And the immortality that Maui sought.
O move to Hawaiki, to the shadow of Io's breath.

No man had died such a death of dreams and storms,
For drowning with memories came that expected devil.
He was racked on the waves and spirit wrecked he wept
For his living sins, each tear-drop swimming with evil.
O soul be chang'd into little water drops
And fall into the ocean ne'er be found!
Dying he shrank from that chief who would seize him
        for ever.

But there no tohunga met him, angels flew
To draw his frightened soul quivering to heaven,
Bright there, bright in the open life of light.

Trying to speak known words that the unbelievers
Might know what was said and bring their ears to Christ,
He had sung with the spirit, prayed with the understanding,
Thus saved the soul he had paid to save the heathen.

His was the plough, he turned the sacred soil
Where others reaped, a pioneer in Christ's
New clearing, strove with unswerving will
Amidst the roots, the rotting stumps and compost
Of the mind to make a bed where the gospel
Might lie down in the breeding sun and grow
A crucifix of leaves, O flowers of crosses.

Immortal in our mouths, and known in heaven,
Yet as we praise we wish him greater—left
On our fractured limb of time, not yet possessed,
Where north will not meet south, of the south's lost gift.
Taught of the sinful flesh he never sensed
That to reach for truth was to reach for God, nor found
God immanent in the cannibals' beliefs.

Father he left us a legacy of guilt,
Half that time owed us, who came from the north,
    was given:
We know St Paul, but what in that dreaming hour,
In that night when the ends of time were tied—
    and severed
Again and so ever—did he learn from the south?
He could not turn to teach his countrymen,
And lost, (our sorrow), lost our birthright for ever.

The Parakeet

Shadows of bars suggest perhaps,
If memory slumbers behind
Those jewelled eyes, eucalypts
Festooned with bark strips, ribboned
With light. But his scream echoes
From farther than Bimberi Peak
Before a word or thought arose
To sing or check the slash of beak.
Clapper in a wire bell, voice
Of a demon in a nun's dream,
Chiming, enticing, then raucous
With a mad, a mindless glee;
His glaze was baked in a volcanic kiln.
Was his the first loudness to rage
Glittering over a slow, reptilian
Earth? Anachronism caged
He sits, a focus of unease—
As though, a sailor's pet, he might
Spout blasphemies to greet the visitors.
Perhaps (his own augur) it is not the light
Of past that keeps him spry: he wakes
Us to an instant's fear that this
May be the sunrise he awaits,
His inheritance of flame, a citrus
Strip in smoking morning, wing-slashed,
And Sydney a screeching desert.

The Young Chess Player

So Orpheus stared, on passing the dog of hell,
Foreseeing milky limbs and cruel, deaf shades;
Or the general, hearing a nightingale while shells
Fell harmlessly, defences well-prepared;
Or Maui, thoughtful, when he felt our weight
Tug from time on his legendary line.
Abstracted, Botticelli-eyed, his sight
Unseeing, he makes in his abstract delight
A future form, where hieroglyphic stars
Wheel to a music singing in his ears.
But these are onlookers' orbits, not the seer's
Awakened images. Perhaps his pure
Designs take flesh or the ghostly form of flesh:
A Persian Queen assaults a Knight with zeal,
But falls before his white, deceptive thrust;
A midnight Bishop slants across a field;
The fainting King surrenders still unhurt;
And all his art is breathless, bleeding action—
His art all struggle, this struggle all his art.
There is only one mystery, a thousand visions—
Who can say (in each man's heavy dream)
If Einstein's incommunicable One
(As each stares blind into his paradigm)
Or this small boy's exact, exacting patterns
Differ from Mallarmé's ice-throttled swan?

KENDRICK SMITHYMAN

Simple Ode

My woman weeping under a bush of stars
twelve points of compass and twelve winds
      I name you
beneath whose halycon gesture moving now
you may stand like a flower tall over
      an earth, a hatred.

To have been a signal flame in time of
desert, the Moses' burning through way through
      torrid exile
      I name you
bird, being loved, whom distance attends on
that flying is light for miles and burning
      bush is the flame
      a fire puts out.

Across these centuries of hostile miles I send
from summer into autumn all my meaning
      with windy approach of leaves
      from a harvest, when armour
      I name you
between the political seasons of danger and
destroying, the days of the weeping woman
between the terror of love and the tremor
history shakes in a bride bed, is making
yet more token of you in your continent yet
not united but in some sad glory trailing
      over my reasonable page
      your fury your story.

Die Bauernhochzeit

He is the victim whom the lean predict
wearing his sad importance on parade
whose special virtue is the awkward stance
who may be led but cannot ever lead.
For Brueghel he made music. Understood
by that old master history commits
his anonymous canvas like a word
which may be said when needed most somewhere
and time assures someone will need to hear.

There with his pipes he watches, slightly drunk
filled with the giggling bawdry of the bedding.
Acquitted of the guilt of those who think
his innocence assumes his painter's sins
and wears them out. His are the neutral lines
subserving pain or power. Does Brueghel
devise with these a text? Is the reading
true sees more than marriage in the bridal?

The piper questions and the indifferent
waiter replies while Brueghel stands behind:
'What is it simply that these people want?'

For all the wind falls on, the suffering
finding daily a surprising light like snow
banked clean on each household after rain,
for the thin trees, strict fingers offering
stringency, for the smooth signal swan,
for all those things which, being, have been,
comets and weddings and admitted pain;
the thrust and the humour and the show
of meaning that was familiar to their homes
they ask evasive morning shall contain.

Anzac Ceremony

That bird that bears our branchy future flies
suddenly from his thicket, and the saddest clown
turning to tell his message of too much grief
puts up his hand for the charity of one leaf,
pleading affection. No one hears or replies.
Will there be never or ever where he may lie down?

I drove my brother bleeding away from my porch.
I, sated, cursed my sister afraid and hungry away.
She took up strength from the blood he gave;
she bound his wound; she brought water to lave
a hurt now healed in them bleeds my reproach.
What difficult word is there which I must say?

Who can forgive me, now being still and alone
with the touch of power, a saintly healing touch?
At their scarred and brothel kiss I cannot balk.
I must walk with the beggar and with the idiot talk;
abandon my goods; my warm bed give to the clown,
that my sister's loss be redeemed as I learn to mumble
   my brother's speech.

Inheritance

Tree, paddock, river: plan
landscape for a child
who will inherit all,
and grow, to be a man—
but when does manhood's wild
ordinance of downfall
first rack him? What the mild
pronouncing deciding year?
five, seven, twenty-one?

How high against the wall
standing knows love and fear
measure him, then undone?
Plan paddock, river, and tree.
The witless agents scan
their amicable sky
but mark fair weather there
where lark and harsh gull fly.
His shadow dulls a stone
outcrop below the track.
A harkaway runs the ridge;
his ewes drift out while clear
morning covers the flat,
pattering feet in the dust.
What morning does he hear
first running at his back
(his heeler, his black bitch)
his silent sedulous pair:
his love, his lovely fear?

from *Considerations*

'High in the Afternoon the Dove'

High in the afternoon the dove
winds melancholy to his mate
a thread of music, monotone
upon the languid afternoon.
The language of his simple love
spills phrases, breaking through the heat.

Heraldic and primeval birds
reflect from their neglected tree
the clemency we did not know,
the charity we could not say,
who kept behind our uncouth words
a terrifying privacy.

Returned to memory they wind
ingenuously, note under note,
our pain commingled with their song,
the pain of music which must hang
like heat stiff on a lazy wind,
stabbing our history to the heart.

After

Put your man down somewhere
in a good lasting soil.
Do not think, bitterly, there
goes the sum of love and toil.

He was so part of you:
you bred him from your fall
into his own; today you endow
your life with his burial.

What was he, this manchild
childman? A doll of stone,
a sop for whatever ailed
you once, a weakness outgrown.

To be Absent Without Leave

Time, sweeping, desolates
your best hours and your hand
stays, short of miracle. You need
look neither far nor hard—the State's
drab agents there demand
your man again to arms;
he's sworn to serve, but not to bleed.

Easterlies cramp the pines,
gorse runs mad on the hill.
Remember me. The game is played
not to be won, but who designs
loss as his aim? I tell
you nothing new; I know
only we are, in time, dismayed.

A Thing Remembered

A thing remembered from some forgotten war,
a trivial thing (which the campaign had bowled
beyond reminiscence, a stuporous earth mould
out of sight for a hundred years) wearing
its yet telltale brain-searing scar
cleaved above the frontal bone—a skull,
purely anonymous, its pure cavity full
only with dirt; distasteful, but enduring.

What is it, to endure? To revive a name
among the unmentionably profane
who inherit us, gene by decrepit gene?
It is nothing, or less, or else should damn
our potency and be our shame.
Brown bone jigged from a conqueror's oven,
it is yours, is it my misgiving unforgiven
I hear whistle sharply while these days cram

rye, wattle, hawthorn, and blackberry
with the sour fruit of merest survival?
Be black, and buried in the pit where charnel
imagining, moping, squats sullen.
Let the imprudent worms marry
in the brain's tenement, their prolix
issue amply use the dome, their colonies wax
fatly fine another century's dissembling:

and then a day. Ghost and shade may we meet
(so fine, they will be seen through at a glance)
at this same funeral ground, the haws' intense
scarlet along the embattled hedge,
that I may pick an armful fit
to show I loved you, knowing that in love
we have compounded faiths our wit will not forgive . . .
This crabbed hawthorn, that was once my clansmen's badge.

Waikato Railstop

Two suicides, not in the one season
    exactly, as we count what is materially
a season: principally I remember for
this railstop a so ordinary quality,
    so neutral, it may be
        distinguished for,

by, what was unusual there, as though
    intensely they cut peepholes through February's
smoke and haze revealing, instantaneous and all-
summing, purest motives, marrying perdition
    with action. Do not, please,
        misrepresent

the hamlet as an enthusiasm
    for the mortuary-minded in a death-centred
democracy. That certain young women should find
themselves unseasonably with child is to be
    understood and even
        an interest

to those on outlying farms. There was also
    an engineer who built an aircraft in his backyard,
which he could not fly; ambition was not licensed
to go soaring. Such an ascent measures most days'
    custom of being flat.
        You may set off

one day from another if you wish or
    if you can, skirting their outlook in the sandy
pinebelts while the Highway on the slight ridge above
consigns traffic elsewhere and a rake of coal-cars
    retreating south does not
        hurry, clacking

into the crossing and out, nor disturbs
    mynahs and bulbuls from their squabbling. Let orchard
and vineyard tally freights of purpose; you do well
or wither and rot where, to entertain your summer
    listening, the child's play
        musketry of

gorsepods fusillades at no target big
    enough to miss. Admiring does not get you far.
Wattleseeds crushed underfoot stink as from a knoll
you track farther across the swamp ravelling out
    and winding mazily
        acres of peat

smoke their signals, but no one, slouching hot,
    cares to separate smoke hulk from thundery cumulus.
Noon massed above blackens cloudland and a cuckold
below, seething skein by skein impartially.
    Outside the billiard room
        a truck backfires.

Parable of Two Talents

Somewhere I read how, long since oh very
Long ago a certain Knight (most certain
In his faith) fought with the Beast
Who was his unbelief, his lack-faith contrary
In all contrarieties; but again,
    Again the Beast would hoist
Himself up from injudiciously being dead
    And not done with
    However he bled,
Stank or staggered, a corrupt patch-pelt
Scurfy verminous draggletail, caricature
    Of piety's detestably impure
Other. And the Knight—how was it he felt?

Variously he felt, variously. There was his pride
Going triumphantly before his fall
With his humility, taxed
Excessive—the Beast was, and could not be, denied.
He felt this way and that while temporal
    Lords, lords spiritual passed
Before him deferential. So he retired
    To a wilderness
    Where his absurd
Pitying servile victim followed him,
His handy monster who sustained him in that place.
    There in his hour Beast washed his tired face,
Digged deep, and chose to die, a lasting whim.

Man and a Brute lie proper in one pit,
Whom warring could not sunder: how deep should
We read the tale? I give it
No commentary, but wonder (an autumn night
Dropping dropping leaves from a dying wood)
    What medieval wit

Intended how far, how much is left unsaid;
    And sit, your virtue's
    Beast, my day not played
Wholly away or so far undone
That I cannot see marriage and this parable
    Could have some truck: you, admirable
And chaste vowed to your Brute. And how alone
Should either face the wilderness who have
So much together fought, so much one mind,
So little understanding,
So much need? Flaunt handsome on your high horse and brave
My scruffy riots; they will again down, bend
    Their craggy knee, commending
Their deathly due the tax of a humbled blood
    night of autumn,
    moonshine pricking the wood
that is a wilderness as I trick
No one (you less than any) with this metaphor
    In which I hide what I should declare
Plainly, a debt that needs no rhetoric.

A Note on the Social Arts

A poem quietly goes aside to weep.
The sulky poet draws his beer and fills
one corner of the bar with flying words
whose wings beat irritable silence in
being birds. Each beak holds a tear
delicious as the christian pearl, yet sullen.
They cry, the birds? but no cry comes.
The pearls roll down. The poet drinks.

My love is a bag of nails, is a bag,
is waiting for me, watching me, is there
outside the street *the barman groans.*

Soon she will tire of me, call Time, she'll move
in step with needless clocks
about the dial of her love to ring
no pressure, then no beer. She pouts, must go
somewhere apart from me to wind her hair
out of another's window till she fall.
I shall be old, dreading to climb and stare.

Round round around the noisy fan glows.
The writer tries his craft. An empty glass.
In a corner stands a poem weeping yet.
The words have talked themselves up to a perch
erratic on a stag's head; where, let pass,
their shades discountenance what mirrors search.
They loom like Furies as the beer goes down.

Someone is singing in the urinal.

Hint for the Incomplete Angler

Not too far north from where I write set dawn
Before your bow precisely. Out there, cast
The kingfish from his feeding while you prey.

Smug blue worms will peck at your neat craft's side.
Show due respect then while you steal the tide.

There was a fisherman once who did things right.

For more than forty years he pulled fish out.
By line, net or pot God's plenty hauled to pout
And puff on the bottomboards, to smack
Themselves silly and die, else were tossed back
Until they swelled a right size for the pan
He kept on the wall by his sink. That man
Had long outgrown the truth of simple tales

Which said if he stroked his arm he showered scales,
That said for years he nourished an old mermaid
All to himself in his bach. Friend, he was staid,
Ordinary, and (it may be) none too bright,
But who could come godlike home with that high light
Morning on morning, to be sane as we
Would claim we are? Yet he did fittingly
More than we'd dream, and with more dignity.

For when he couldn't heave any more at the net,
When the old man snapper clung too hard, he set
His nose to the sea away out east of the Head
To give what was due from good years to the tide.

Watch for the worms as you go, at your dinghy's side.

Blackleg

Careering on a downslope from the bail,
it was myself, in part it was myself
committed to the pothole, steep
sickening rumbledumble with a fly's
lewd concert at the end. Such a close
to round one only summer, and be dung
or even less than dung: a dissolution
of the parts corporal, their incorporeal arts.

In the holding yard where the calves guzzled
tippling skim milk, pattering, I bawled
that he was found the missing one,
him offered to arbitrary summer
where one by one or squadrons at a whim
thistles discharged their flights.
Gauze in a fine wearing, but the yard
unhallowed; he must have been lying

all through the day near the trough
coarsening—you know how the eyes are,
looking past seeing and not looking,
his near forequarter swollen blackly.
Or the tongue, although it is not
detail which quickens remembering,
the masculine pouch prematurely
unrealized, the not-meditative horns.

While wood pigeons grossly fed on
karaka berries, exulting appetite,
I looped a chain about the hindlegs,
the Thing in his unbecoming I dragged
down the slope to a pothole which had
been abandoned by the Forest stream,
there resigned him
to be forgotten. And washed my hands
where the pool blinks with native trout.

It was February in nineteen thirty-nine.
I was old enough and too young to know
that exceptions breed like flies,
but what is to be imported
in a commonplace? The younger bulls
in their simplicity sported the paddock.

Night-Piece

Late, of a late summer night, almost white
with being still, highway sounds remote
like assurance of land looming not quite seen
which surrounds a lake where you go
as though stalking the water, and the lawn is
dew damp, the air is leaning into autumn
a shade more than cool less than cold.

Light among trees there, a neighbour's tenor
strangled in his shower box, an irrelevant
dialogue of the insects of our darkness.
It is too soon to go to bed. The crickets scratch
meticulously at what your moon makes smooth.

To be alone is what you pay for peace.
It is too soon to try for sleep, but staying
awake is lying at the mercy of darkness
in a room of many faces, heavy-eyed.
We are blamed in our generation.
All I have learned is how to fail differently.

HONE TUWHARE

Lament [1]

In that strident summer of battle
    when cannon grape and ball
    tore down the pointed walls
    and women snarled as men
    and blood boiled in the eyes:
    in the proud winter of defeat
    he stood unweary
    and a god among men.

He it was whom death looked hotly on
    whilst I in adoration
    brought timid fuel to his fire:
    of all things manly he partook

yet did it plummet down like a bird
    engulfing him as he headlong
    rushed towards the night:
    the long night
    where no dawn wakes to pale
    the quaking stars: farewell

Farewell companion of laughter and light
    who warmed the nights with the
    croaking chants of olden times: hear
    me now sing poorly sing harshly. . . .

At dawn's light I looked for you
    at the land's end where two oceans froth
    but you had gone without leaving a sign
    or a whispered message to the gnarled
    tree's feet or the grass or the inscrutable
    rock face. Even the innocent day-dreaming
    moon could not explain the wind's wry mirth.

[1] Suggested by a tangi in Sir George Grey's *Nga Moteatea*.

To you it seems I am nothing—
    a nobody and of little worth
    whom the disdainful years
    neither praise nor decry
    but shall abandon to fat
    and the vast delight of worms: farewell

Farewell farewell
    Let the heavens mumble and stutter
    Let them acknowledge your leaving us
    Mine is the lone gull's cry in the night
    Let my grief hide the moon's face
    Let alien gods salute thee
    with flashing knives cut open
    the dark belly of the sky.

    I feel rain spit in my face

I bear no malice, let none stain my valedictions
For I am at one with the wind
    the clouds' heave and the slapping rain
    the tattered sky and the wild solitude
    of the sea and the streaming earth
    which I kneel to kiss. . . .

Burial

    In a splendid sheath
    of polished wood and glass
    with shiny appurtenances
    lay he fitly blue-knuckled
    and serene:

    hurry rain and trail him
    to the bottom of the grave

Flowers beyond budding
will not soften the gavel's
beat of solemn words
and hard sod thudding:

hurry rain and seek him
at the bottom of the grave

Through a broken window
inanely looks he up;
his face glass-gouged and bloodless
his mouth engorging clay
for all the world uncaring. . . .

Cover him quickly, earth!
Let the inexorable seep of rain
finger his greening bones, deftly.

The Old Place

No one comes
by way of the doughy track
through straggly tea tree bush
and gorse, past the hidden spring
and bitter cress.

Under the chill moon's light
no one cares to look upon
the drunken fence-posts
and the gate white with moss.

No one except the wind
saw the old place
make her final curtsy
to the sky and earth:

and in no protesting sense
did iron and barbed wire
ease to the rust's invasion
nor twang more tautly
to the wind's slap and scream.

On the cream-lorry
or morning paper van
no one comes,
for no one will ever leave
the golden city on the fussy train;
and there will be no more waiting
on the hill beside the quiet tree
where the old place falters
because no one comes any more

no one.

The Girl in the Park

The girl in the park
    saw a nonchalant sky
    shrug into a blue-dark
    denim coat.

    The girl in the park
    did not reach up to touch
    the cold steel buttons.

The girl in the park
    saw the moon glide
    into a dead tree's arms
    and felt the vast night
    pressing.
    How huge it seems,
    and the trees are big she said.

The stars heard her
and swooped down perching
on tree-top and branch
owl-like and unblinking.

The grave trees,
as muscular as her lover
leaned darkly down to catch
the moonrise and madness
in her eyes:
the moon is big, it is very big
she said with velvet in her throat.

An owl hooted.
The trees scraped and nudged
each other and the stars
carried the helpless
one-ribbed moon away. . . .

The girl in the park
does not care: her body swaying
to the dark-edged chant
of storms.

Muscle and Bone of Song

And of trees and the river
no more say
that these alone are sources
for the deft song and the sad:
nor from wave-curl and the sun
cross moon wind and hail
calm and storm come.

Joyously I sing
to the young girl's hip-knock

and taunt: swing-cheerful breasts
shape my hands
to eternal begging-bowls.

Rain

I can hear you making
small holes in the silence
rain

If I were deaf
the pores of my skin
would open to you
and shut

And I should know you
by the lick of you
if I were blind:

the steady drum-roll
sound you make
when the wind drops

the something
special smell of you
when the sun cakes
the ground

But if I should not
hear
smell or feel or see you

you would still
define me
disperse me
wash over me
rain

LOUIS JOHNSON

Magpie and Pines

That dandy black-and-white gentleman doodling notes
on fragrant pinetops over the breakfast morning,
has been known to drop through mists of bacon-fat,
with a gleaming eye, to the road where a child stood, screaming.

And in the dark park—the secretive trees—have boys
harboured their ghosts, built huts, and buried treasure,
and lovers made from metallic kisses alloys
more precious, and driven the dark from pleasure.

A child was told that bird as his guardian angel
reported daily on actions contrived to displease;
stands petrified in the sound of wings, a strangle
of screams knotting his throat beneath the winter leaves.

Look back and laugh on the lovers whose white mating
made magpie of dark; whose doodling fingers swore
various fidelities and fates. They found the world waiting,
and broke the silence. A raven croaks 'Nevermore'

to their progenitive midnight. The guardian is aloof
on his roof of the small world, composing against morning
a new, ironic ballad. The lover has found small truth
in the broken silence, in faith, or the fate-bird moaning.

New Worlds for Old

'New worlds for old,' sings the golden-fisted youth
Smashing the morning into a myriad stars
To wind in his girl's dark hair, pin on her mouth
In lightning kisses set to glimmer there.

New worlds for old he promises, and takes
The blind blank windows of her life and fills
The garden with dreamseed, shocks and shakes
Fruit from the tree—forbidden, so it thrills.

And looking out, she will not recognize
The formal pattern under the new leaves,
But think that flame of flowers the true size
Of his earthshaking manhood: so she believes

His shape and slogan as he grows and sings
'New worlds for old!' And true, it's changing fast.
There is a thickness in the voice that wings
With less abandon among echoes past.

'Old worlds for new!' the note is tremolo.
The old man quavering is grey with tears.
Is it his voice, or a youth beneath the window
Smashing the morning with promise that he hears?

Here Together Met

I praise Saint Everyman, his house and home
  In every paint-bright gardened suburb shining
With all the age's verities and welcome
  Medalled upon him in contentment dining;
            And toast with gin and bitters
            The Muse of baby-sitters.

I sing Dame Everyone's whose milky breast
  Suckles the neighbourhood with pins and plans
Adding new rooms to their eternal rest,
  The next night's meat already in the pan:
            And toast with whisky and ice,
            The Goddess who keeps things nice.

207

I honour Maid Anybody's whose dreams are shaping
    Lusts in her heart down the teasing garden-path
Where she stops in time as she must at the gaping
    Graveyard of Hell and rescues her girlish laugh:
            And toast in rum and cloves
            The course of balanced *love.*

I drink to Son Mostpeople's whose honourable pride
    In things being what they are will not let him run,
But who keeps things going even after he has died
    In a distant desert clutching an empty gun:
            And toast in brandy and lime
            The defenders of our great good time.

from *Four Poems from the Strontium Age*

I

Before the Day of Wrath

There were cities here in the hills
In my great-grandfather's youth
Where now are only blackened bricks and walls
Devoured in the year of wrath.

And in the desert where none of us
Dare venture, hearing tell
Of fabulous, dangerous monsters, flowers
Were said to emerge when rare rain fell.

Today the rain draws blood; the winds
Burn out our eyes; the barbarous
Plants tear flesh that never mends:
Sweet water-holes turn suddenly poisonous.

It must have been a lovely country once,
Populous and inventive—a golden age
Wherein the young knew laughter, loved to dance,
Even grew old. Daylight as bright as courage

Existed for many hours at a time, we're told.
But these, perhaps, are fables meant to inspire
Us now in the darkness helping us to hold
Something to cherish crouched by the guttering fire.

3

Spring

All day the black rain has fallen
And now, in the hour of light
The livid river and the lake are swollen;
The range of hills that were bright

And red with their carpet of dust
Are dissolving away. Soon there will be
No shelter: again we must
Pack and move in search of kinder country.

Then will begin again that dread migration
Through sightless deserts, and the silent land
Reflecting sickness into our eyes, starvation
Bloating the children with its grotesque hand.

And never knowing which way is the best
To set the foot because the perils met there
Can never be foreseen nor wholly guessed,
For who can tell what colour of the air

Harbours most pain? Surely the Spring
Is the most bitter season of suffering.

4

Haven

We have come to a quiet valley in the hills
Where a road, this time unbroken, runs
Right back to the desert fringe. It fills
Us with a dreaming hope. The sun's

Mild light is clean; about and above
The slopes are grassy. In our ears
The little river sings a song like love.
In the old country, for two thousand years

There ruled a king called God, the story goes.
It seems impossible, but here is a place
Where one might trust to fable. Flowers grow
And trees stand straight beside the watercourse.

Let us not be afraid. After two days and nights
In such a haven, we fear that we may have brought
With us those breeding poisons of the world's blight
That will blacken the earth here and pollute the light.

And already the leaders confer in the common interest,
And it's rumoured that they plan to eliminate
The sickliest and those of us who are least
Like men should be. Oh, may we all grow straight

In this place of the sun. Let me not think of these
Cruel facts of life in this valley of green trees.

Bread and a Pension

It was not our duty to question but to guard,
maintaining order; see that none escaped
who may be required for questioning by the State.
The price was bread and a pension and not a hard
life on the whole. Some even scraped
enough on the side to build up a fairish estate

for the day of retirement. I never could
understand the complaints of the restless ones
who found the hours long, time dragging;
it always does. The old hands knew how good
the guardroom fire could be, the guns
gleaming against the wall and the nagging

wind like a wife—outside. There were cards
for such occasions and good companions
who truly were more than home since they shared
one's working life without difference or hard words,
aimed at much the same thing, and shared opinions
on news they read. If they cared

much it was for the quiet life. You cannot hold
that against them, since it's roundly human
and any decent man would want it the same.
For these were decent: did as they were told,
fed prisoners, buried the dead, and, on occasion
loaded the deathcart with those who were sent to the flames.

Matter of Urgency

Most prefer not to know, proceed by faith and chance
Between one day and the next; but he
Had been given his passport—had one year to live—
And could not afford the casual, passing glance
In the face of that journey. Each activity
Now must count, each minute be made to give.

There was nothing stoical in the face he turned
To hail the morning, but a measured welcome
Like Midas counting his money, and reaching out
To transform another deliberate rose. The bond
Between his hand and each object became
So strong he could give nothing up, nor surrender to doubt.

He became obsessed by minutiae; would sit
By the hour observing flies at their rituals,
Noting the motes in sunbeams, but could not bring
His forces down on what once had seem important—
To tidy his papers, enter up all the journals
And leave his desk in order for his going.

Disorder was, in fact, a thing he'd survived,
And he could not bear to appear uncharacteristic;
There were always others to edit, care for such matters
More expert and better paid than himself. He thrived
In his final idleness: shaved daily, enjoyed breakfast
And took out the scraps and crumbs to feed to the sparrows.

He Smelt the Smell of Death Within the Marrow

Waking one morning, he was alarmed to find
he had a different odour, riper and more
unpleasant than he had ever noticed before;
bodily or a characteristic of mind
he could not be sure though he tried
to trace the spot exactly. It did not seem
to bother others unduly: it was the dream
of himself, he found, that died
and added to his disgust. And even though
he walked more finically, washed more often,
took greater pains all round it would not soften
the fact. It was like learning to live with a blow
that landed and stunned one every seventh minute;
and then—it scarcely surprised him—he did not appear
to wear the same face any more but one vaguer
as though he were copying something and within it
tried to maintain an act prescribed by someone
he was no longer in touch with. Gradually
this indefinition began to appear as an ally—
giving him less to dislike—allowing the run
of the luck to change. Again he could stand
and assess the claims of the passing girls though he did
not fully believe that act any more and hid
his fear under many conquests, birds in the hand
meaning more than hopes in the hush of himself.
He saw God as a deodorant on a completely immaculate shelf.

What his friends noticed most was an indrawn air
pinching the nostrils; he did not laugh so much
as they remembered; and there was a touch
of distance about him.
                    He was more mature,
they consoled themselves, and never sensed the throes
he went through daily under their very noses.

The Birthday

The old man is a greyer stone this year
the morning of his fifty-seventh birthday:
a sputtering gaiety among defining
clocks, the blessing fingers of grandchildren:

and it's a small score in the accountancy
of history: simply a private matter
with little jokes, familiar knives and cups
and the same circle of faces to testify:

the tokens are scarcely a harvest—rather
a minor festival of little people poised
between the murder of years in time
like a wave at the ends of worlds

that will rise, engulf them, drown
eyes, hands, around the table of smiles,
same cups and knives and faces saying
(in spite of skies that fall) our father.

The Perfect Symbol

I remember reading as a boy, Giotto,
Asked for a picture fit for a Pope's wall,
Picked up a brush, painted a perfect circle,
And offered this as prize to the puzzled pontiff
Whose shocked reaction was a dark reproof.
'No, sir,' the painter answered, 'Nothing less
Than this would be apt gift for your great grace.
This line is endless and begins nowhere.

It contains all the truth a man might know
And is a barrier excluding dross.
Or, it's a world, and outside it, the heavens
And every aspiration worthy of him.
I made it with one stroke: you cannot tell
Where I began it, only that, through grace,
Patience, the pain of all my craft,
I made what Nature does not make—the circle,
The thing enclosed, entire, perfection's symbol.'

Humbled, his master gave it pride of place
Upon the palace wall, and no doubt gave
Much thought as well to what might burn within
A peasant breast that beat beyond itself
In realms of contemplation learning strove for
Without, always, the same degrees of insight.
Then let Giotto's circle stand for those
Who see beyond the lines and shapes of things,
The orders, and the ordering of men's lives,
And all the passing show, to what might be
Ultimate truths contained in a simple act,
The maker's hand unveiling what is hidden
From understanding by what's understood,
And what is real surprisingly revealed,
Hard, simple, whole, something to stand for ever.

JANET FRAME

Yet Another Poem About a Dying Child

Poets and parents say he cannot die
so young, so tied to trees and stars.
Their word across his mouth obscures
and cures his murmuring good-bye.
He babbles, *they say*, of spring flowers,

who for six months has lain
his flesh at a touch bruised violet,
his face pale, his hate clearer
than milky love that would smooth over
the pebbles of diseased bone.

Pain spangles him like the sun,
He cries and cannot say why.
His blood blossoms like a pear tree.
He does not want to eat or keep
its ugly windfall fruit.

He does not want to spend or share
the engraved penny of light
that birth put in his hand
telling him to hold it tight.
Will parents and poets not understand?

He must sleep, rocking the web of pain
till the kind furred spider will come
with the night-lamp eyes and soft tread
to wrap him warm and carry him home
to a dark place, and eat him.

At Evans Street

I came one day upon a cream-painted wooden house
with a white bargeboard, a red roof, two gates,
two kinds of japonica bushes, one gooseberry bush,
one apple tree lately in blossom; and thus I counted
my fortune in gates and flowers, even in the white
bargeboard and the fallen roofbeam crying religiously
    to the carpenter,
Raise me high! and in this part of the city that would
    be
high indeed for here my head is level with hills and sky.

It is not unusual to want somewhere to live but the
     impulse
bears thinking about seriously and it is wise
never to forget the permanent impermanence of the
    grave,
its clay floor, the molten centre of the earth, its untiled
roof, the rain and sunbeams arrowing through slit
windows and doors too narrow to escape through,
locked by the remote control of death-bed convulsions
in a warm room in a cream-painted wooden house with
a red roof, a white bargeboard, fallen roofbeam . . .
        no, it is not unusual
to nest at my time of year and life only it is wisest
to keep the spare room always for that unexpected guest,
    mortality,
whose tall stories, growing taller, tell
of the sea-gull dwelling on bare cliffs, of eagles high
where the bailiff mountain wind removes all furniture
    (had eagles known the need
for chairs by the fireside—what fire but the sun?) and
    strips the hangings
from the trees; and the men, also, camouflaged as trees,
    who climb the rock
face and of the skylark

217

from whose frenzied point of view harvest is hurricane
and when
except in the world of men
did hurricanes provide shelter and food?

In my house I eat bread and wish the guest would go.

The Clown

His face is streaked with prepared tears.
I, with others, applaud him, knowing it
is fashionable to approve when a clown cries
and to disapprove when a persistent sourface
does whether or not his tears are paint.

It is also fashionable, between wars,
to say that hate is love and love is hate,
to make out everything is more complex than we dreamed
and then to say we did not dream it,
we knew it all along and are wise.

Dear crying clown dear childlike old man
dear kind murderer dear innocent guilty
dear simplicity I hate you for making me pretend
there are several worlds to one truth when
I know, I know there are not. Dear people like you and me
whose breaths are bad, who sleep in and rumble
their bowels and control it until
they get home into the empty house or among the family
dear family, dear lonely man in torn world of nobody,
is it for this waste that we have hoarded words over so many
million years since the first, groan,
and look up at the stars. Oh oh the sky is too wide to sleep under!

Rain on the Roof

My nephew sleeping in a basement room
has put a sheet of iron outside his window
to recapture the sound of rain falling on the roof.

I do not say to him, The heart has its own comfort for grief.
A sheet of iron repairs roofs only. As yet unhurt by the demand
that change and difference never show, he is still able
to mend damages by creating the loved rain-sound
he thinks he knew in early childhood.

Nor do I say, In the travelling life of loss
iron is a burden, that one day he must find
within himself in total darkness and silence
the iron that will hold not only the lost sound of the rain
but the sun, the voices of the dead, and all else that has gone.

Wet Morning

Though earthworms are so cunningly contrived
without an opposing north and south wind
to blow the bones of Yes apart from the flesh of No,
yet in speech they are dumbly overturning,
in morning flood they are always drowned.

This morning they are trapped under the apple tree
by rain as wet as washing-day is wet and dry.
An abject way for the resilient anchorage of trees,
the official précis of woman and man,
the mobile pillarbox of history, to die!

When the Sun Shines More Years Than Fear

When the sun shines more years than fear
when birds fly more miles than anger
when sky holds more bird
sails more cloud
shines more sun
than the palm of love carries hate,
even then shall I in this weary
seventy-year banquet say, Sunwaiter,
Birdwaiter, Skywaiter,
I have no hunger,
remove my plate.

ALISTAIR CAMPBELL

from *Elegy*

2

Now he is Dead

Now he is dead, who talked
Of wild places and skies
Inhabited by the hawk;

Of the hunted hare that flies
Down bare parapets of stone,
And there closes its eyes;

Of trees fast-rooted in stone
Winds bend but cannot break;
Of the low terrible moan

That dead thorn trees make
On a windy desolate knoll;
Of the storm-blackened lake

Where heavy breakers roll
Out of the snow-bred mist,
When the glittering air is cold;

Of the Lion Rock that lifts
Out of the whale-backed waves
Its black sky-battering cliffs;

Of the waterfall that raves
Down the dark mountain side,
And into a white cauldron dives.

The Laid-out Body

Now grace, strength and pride
Have flown like the hawk;
The mind like the spring tide,

Beautiful and calm; the talk;
The brilliance of eye and hand;
The feet that no longer walk.

All is new, and all strange—
Terrible as a dusty gorge
Where a great river sang.

Daisy Pinks

O catch Miss Daisy Pinks
Undressing behind her hair;
She slides open like a drawer
Oiled miraculously by a stare.

O the long cool limbs,
The ecstatic shot of hair,
And untroubled eyes
With their thousand mile stare.

Her eyes are round as marigolds,
Her navel drips with honey,
Her pulse is even, and her laugh
Crackles like paper money.

Hut Near Desolated Pines

Cobwebs and dust have long
Deadened an old man's agony.
The choked fireplace, the chair
On its side on the mud floor,
May have warmed an old man's
Bones or propped them upright
While his great head nodded;
Fantastical images may have stirred
His mind when the wind moaned
And sparks leapt up the chimney
With a roar. But what great gust
Of the imagination threw wide
The door and smashed the lamp
And overturned both table and chair . . . ?
A rabbiter found him sprawled
By the door—no violence, nothing
To explain, but the hungry rats
That scurried over the fouled straw.
A foolish lonely old man
With his whiskers matted with dung.
Since when birds have stuffed the chimney
With straw, and a breeze flapped
Continually through the sack window;
And all the while the deft spiders
Doodled away at their obituaries,
And the thin dust fell from the rafters . . .
Nothing but cobwebs and dust
Sheeting an old man's agony.

At a Fishing Settlement

October, and a rain-blurred face,
And all the anguish of that bitter place.
It was a bare sea-battered town,
With its one street leading down
On to a shingly beach. Sea winds
Had long picked the dark hills clean
Of everything but tussock and stones
And pines that dropped small brittle cones
On to a soured soil. And old houses flanking
The street hung poised like driftwood planking
Blown together and could not outlast
The next window-shuddering blast
From the storm-whitened sea.
It was bitterly cold; I could see
Where muffled against gusty spray
She walked the clinking shingle; a stray
Dog whimpered and pushed a small
Wet nose into my hand—that is all.
Yet I am haunted by that face,
That dog, and that bare bitter place.

Aunt Lucrezia

A Portrait

Yes. Such were the eyes through which in rage and pain
Coiled the spent zodiac of her spirit;
And skin that tarnished where a finger rubbed it,
And jewelled boneless hand that stroked a ferret.

And mark the enamelled mouth, the ears laid back
Bitch-like against a head whose pride appalled
(Despite the coiffeur's art) my uncles most of all:
The head beneath the wig rose clear and bald.

The approving eye unerringly alights
On formal trees as fine as maidenhair,
Takes in a tower, moves upwards to interrogate
A hawk and pigeon circling in the air

Behind her. A day as lucid as the brows
For which ironic loves expend their breath,
Brandy behind their ears, brandy on their breath—
O subtle miniaturist in violent death!

—As I remarked, the head was bald . . . as glass,
And was especially odious to my uncles
To whom all forms of glass breathed and were evil;
The eye inhales the jug, dilates and rankles

Where Lucrezia's hand, boneless as a mollusc,
Slips in a phial, winks, and disappears,
As do my uncles and all their heirs . . .
The jewelled hands play with the ferret's ears.

Looking at Kapiti

Sleep, Leviathan, shouldering the Asian
Night sombre with fear, kindled by one star
Smouldering through fog, while the goaded ocean
Recalls the fury of Te Rauparaha.

Massive, remote, familiar, hung with spray,
You seem to guard our coast, sanctuary
To our lost faith, as if against the day
Invisible danger drifts across the sea.

And yet in the growing darkness you lose
Your friendly contours, taking on the shape
Of the destroyer—dread Moby Dick whose
Domain is the mind, uncharted, without hope.

Without hope I watch the dark envelop
You and like a light on a foundering ship's
Masthead the star go out, while shoreward gallop
The Four Horsemen of the Apocalypse.

My Mother

Rebellion was in her character.
Sullenly beautiful, of *ariki*
Descent, childbearing utterly wrecked her,
So that she died young in Tahiti
Where she was buried. (There's a snapshot
Of her flower-strewn grave, with my sister,
Morose with grief, beside it.) I forgot
To cry, being puzzled, but later missed her.

Sleepless tonight in hospital I search
My memory, but I can find no trace
Of that rebellion, yet like a damp torch
It smouldered in her, lighting up her face
With unearthly beauty. What was its name
If not tuberculosis of the womb?

Wild Honey

Stuart's gallantry . . . I recall how once
he beat a bully who had called his girl
some mildly offensive name . . . *Wild honey.*

Margaret's passion . . . She danced a hula once,
for a Director of Education,
on a cluttered supper board . . . *Wild honey.*

Lilburn's solitude . . . Alone he paces
an empty beach, creating in his head
bare harmonies of sand and wave . . . *Wild honey.*

Meg's loveliness . . . In that absurd boatshed
how it glowed, while the tide chuckled and slapped
below us—God, how she glowed! . . . *Wild honey.*

These things: gallantry, passion, solitude,
and loveliness—how they glow! . . . *Wild honey.*

The Return

And again I see the long pouring headland,
And smoking coast with the sea high on the rocks,
The gulls flung from the sea, the dark wooded hills
Swarming with mist, and mist low on the sea.

And on the surf-loud beach the long spent hulks,
The mats and splintered masts, the fires kindled
On the wet sand, and men moving between the fires,
Standing or crouching with backs to the sea.

Their heads finely shrunken to a skull, small
And delicate, with small black rounded beaks;
Their antique bird-like chatter bringing to mind
Wild locusts, bees, and trees filled with wild honey—

And, sweet as incense-clouds, the smoke rising, the fire
Spitting with rain, and mist low with rain—
Their great eyes glowing, their rain-jewelled, leaf-green
Bodies leaning and talking with the sea behind them,

Plant gods, tree gods, gods of the middle world . . . Face down-
    ward
And in a small creek mouth all unperceived,
The drowned Dionysus, sand in his eyes and mouth,
In the dim tide lolling—beautiful, and with the last harsh

Glare of divinity from lip and broad brow ebbing . . .
The long-awaited! And the gulls passing over with shrill cries;
And the fires going out on the thundering sand;
And the mist, and the mist moving over the land.

Bitter Harvest

The big farm girl with the dumb prophetic body
And shoulders plump and white as a skinned peach
Goes singing through the propped-up apple boughs.

Behind her steps an ancient Jersey cow
With bones like tent-poles and udder swinging.

And last a hairy boy who with a fishing-pole
Drives youth and age before him, flanked by boulders
More yielding than his love. O bitter harvest

When drought affirms and plenitude denies!
Well, let them pass. Assuredly the boy
Will drop his worm into a dusty hole

And fish up . . . death, and the ancient cow
On which so much depends will clear the moon.

Blue Rain

Blue rain from a clear sky.
Our world a cube of sunlight—
but to the south
the violet admonition
of thunder.

Innocent as flowers,
your eyes with their thick lashes
open in green surprise.

What have we to fear?
Frost and a sharp wind
reproach us,
and a tall sky pelts the roof
with blue flowers.

You and I in bed, my love,
heads leaning together,
merry as thieves
eating stolen honey—
what have we to fear
but a borrowed world
collapsing all about us
in blue ruins?

Why Don't You Talk to Me?

Why do I post my love letters
in a hollow log?
Why put my lips to a knothole in a tree
and whisper your name?

The spiders spread their nets
and catch the sun,
and by my foot in the dry grass
ants rebuild a broken city.
Butterflies pair in the wind,
and the yellow bee,
his holsters packed with bread,
rides the blue air like a drunken cowboy.

More and more I find myself
talking to the sea.
I am alone with my footsteps.
I watch the tide recede,
and I am left with miles of shining sand.

Why don't you talk to me?

Gathering Mushrooms

Dried thistles hide his face.
Look closely—
that's your enemy.
Ants carry away his flesh,
but still he grins.
You know him by his thumbs,
round and white,
breaking the earth like mushrooms,
coated with fine sand.

A bony finger flicks a bird
into your face,
daisies snap at your heels,
nostrils
flare in the ground
that you believed was solid—
and a dark wind rides
the whinnying tussock up the hillside.

Gather your mushrooms then,
and, if you dare,
ignore the thin cries of the damned
issuing through the gills.

Sick of running away,
you drop in the soaking grass.
Through tears
you watch a snail climbing a straw
that creaks and bends
under its weight,
and note how tenderly it lifts
upon its shoulder
the fallen weight of the sky.

Purple Chaos

'Chaos is purple,' you said.
'A painter's phrase,' I said,
disagreeing.
'Chaos is a colourless force
tossing up stars, flowers
and children,
and has no beginning
and no end.'

But lying in bed,
washed up,
I know you are right.
You were talking of something else—
You were talking of death.
Purple chaos has surged through me,
leaving me stranded—
a husk,
an empty shell
on a long white swerving beach.

Something has died,
something precious has died.
It may have been a flower,
a star,
it may have been a child—
but whatever it was, my love,
it seems to have died.

The Gunfighter

You will see him any day in Te Kuiti
or Cannons Creek,
immaculate in black
and triggered like a panther on the prowl.

Conscious of all eyes,
but indifferent to all except the heroine
watching from behind lace curtains,
doom walks the main street of a small town.

Is it fear or admiration that widens
those lovely eyes?
He knows her eyes are on him,
but gives no sign he knows—
he has a job to do.

The sun has reached high noon.
The shadows stand with flattened palms
against the walls of buildings,
or shrink back into doorways.
The heroine lets fall the curtain.
She has fallen—
drilled clean through the heart with love.

Now he stands alone
in the pool of his own shadow,
his wrists flexible as a dancing girl's,
his palms hovering like butterflies
over the blazing butts of his sixguns.

The streets are cleared,
the township holds its breath—
for the gunfighter, the terrible gunfighter
is in town.

W. H. OLIVER

In the Fields of My Father's Youth

1

In the fields of my father's youth, now bountiful and green,
I walked and stared, half-recollecting each
New but anticipated emblem of a past
once legendary, now more remote than legend,
remembering all he had told for the delight of children:
folk-habits, succession of seasons and lives,
the dim procession of my ancestors
walking through centuries this treadmill lane.

Its trench between stone bramble-plaited hedges
wound where the contour made a passage easy,
past fertile hills where he had worked all seasons,
last of the peasant line who broke this earth.
Mill and manor, farm house, cottages,
kept up an easy, sociable conversation:
a discourse of rank and degree, proud and humble
linked by its cautious line in a common life.

I celebrated every moderate hope
that lay embedded in the lane's hard clay
feeling myself made radical once more;
and celebrated, too, the manor house,
crown of the country, elegant, discreet
as well-worn riches, sweet as piety.

2

How many hopes were trenched in the secretive lane?
I populated every crossroad with
a host of suicides impaled on hate:
passionate, modest, impossible hopes, denied
in life and death the four unwinding roads
which lead, whichever way, to difference.

When it was moonlight, how many bones
jangled together at Black Cross and White Cross
as an army of lost liberators gaped for flesh?
How great a multitude of dreams? Not his,
at the end. They leapt across an era and a world and pitched
full-flighted, ready to flower, on an empty island,
travelled the dust and gravel of a new highroad
linking, not age to age, but moderate hope to hope.

Solitude, dream, their pinched and starving hopes,
his and my ancestors', he brought to breed
in the raw clay and timber of a settlement
new and elsewhere; not anywhere
the manor's grace could mock their stuntedness.

3

His dream is fulfilled in an acre of fertile ground;
took body in a house, a family;
in leisure, fruit and flowers, company;
work winning ease, children bringing home
children for grandparents, warmth for autumn.
The dream is fulfilled in an empty island town,
a street of stucco shops and iron verandas
perched on the site of a violated forest;
a temporary borough pitiable
beneath the winter snow range meditating
flood and disaster in the final spring—
not yet. Clay gapes in cuttings and the soil runs down
each winter river; land is dying; yet
there will be life in it enough for him,
enough for the dream to flourish and express
a permanent hope lodged in impermanence,
given, in one brief life, a chance to live
apart from that perpetual English rite:
one taken chance, then newness, all things strange.

Till that time fall from the mountain and the sky
I think the innumerable peasantry within
his hand and eye, the ground bass of that theme
particular skill and courage elaborate,
are strong and sappy in his acre garden
and, I expect, are happy as never on earth
moving in his disguises among strawberry frames,
directing the growth of flowers round a house.
They are prodigal there who died in paucity
and, having raised a county's fodder and crops,
delight themselves in more luxurious harvests.

And I think they talk through the words of poetry
he writes to me here in England, telling me
of the growth and profit and joy of his fruitful acre
as once in passion and in oratory
they stood on platform, soapbox, with the jobless,
full of the argument of state, rebelliously
talking down privilege, arguing equal rights.
That dream flower faded, cynically abused;
the song of equality became a bribe
offered abroad by immoral political apes,
while good men reeled in the wake of procureurs.

There is only the garden full of surprising fruit.

4

The lane led away to the by-pass, to the rail,
to the university town, this desk, these words.
Can I who live by his flight relinquish either
the peasant's dream or the eloquent manor house?
Both were his first and every birthday gift.

All those who sleep in tears within my seed
will reach, if I do not, the breaking point
where loyalties depart and go their ways
separate, hostile, taking up their arms
to meet in battle on the disputed field
of England's and our own heart's heritage.

That will be time for treasons and for faith.

RAYMOND WARD

Watching Snow

You were standing at the window, silently
when the first flakes began to fall
between the houses, to settle in the boughs
of the leafless elm and in the yard below;
and so intently were you watching them
spin through the early winter gloom
to catch in fences, heap the window sill,
you did not notice when I spoke to you.

So I fell silent, too. But no,
not just because the snow enchanted me:
the way you stood there like a memory
re-awakened so much tenderness
I had thought buried long ago,
nostalgic, maternal as the falling snow,
that I was glad when you made no reply.
Nearness enough to watch you standing there,

and as intently as you watched the snow:
it gathered slowly, darkening your hair
and shoulders, till your outline only, drained
like a negative, at last remained,
sharp against the window veiled with steam.
You must have known that I was watching you,
pierced by the memory a snowflake clears,
or why were you also, when you turned, in tears?

Ode to an Urban Day

The urban day has got her blue straw hat on
the one with the yellow rose in it
and her grey eyes beneath it
are cool and smiling.

238

Wherever the streets go
and there are people
her walk is leisurely:

in the early morning she stands in the shade
in the park at noon she will feed the pigeons
in the evening she will wave good-bye to us—

you understand,
she is not working very hard today,
she is there to look pretty.

In her dove-grey dress
she is warm but not uncomfortable
and she is not dusty:
late last night she had a shower
and another this morning;
so her skin is fresh
and her breath sweet.

From time to time she pauses—
before shop windows and pools of rain
to admire her reflection,
then, smiling, strolls on.
She is lovely today
and she knows it:

she will stand at bus stops
and wait. Although the buses pull up
she remains where she is—
she does not mind when people stare
she does not think them indiscreet.

If one tries to take her photograph
she laughs,
for she is always changing
and no camera has a nose.

She does not belong to us.
We belong to her,
no matter what mood she is in.
But we must not ignore her—
to remain is not enough.

Evening is the time, if any, for departure
but today she does not wish to leave us
nor does she wish to see us leave:

she stands there in her faded blue straw hat
looking for the rose—which must have come untied,
as if to say, would someone be so kind . . . ?

then she begins to wander
in and out of doorways
from one street to the next . . .

but we have lost her now
grey as the corner she is huddled into
for the night,

still sweet, her fragrance lingers
in the pool of night rain
where the rose has fallen . . .

Intimacy

The house nailed up and boarded in
by a tall fence of rain;
drab windows laced with steam
and in the corners of the ceiling
twilight of a stormy afternoon.
No calls anticipated.
Gone from the mantelpiece the clock:
for once time will not tell,
safely bound in the bottom drawer
and gagged with a bedsock.

Solo for Clarinet

I am always meeting him. In his rags
or in his extra special clothes, he
lands on both feet from out of nowhere.
Like new.
        A springy disconcerting number
with a slouch hat skimming one ear
like a spun lariat, or a tray load
tilting on a waiter's palm;
alternatively, rubbed right forward
astonishing his nose.
        Definitely
not the man-in-the-street. Not
Everyman. Nothing like that.
Himself: as water is inclined
to be liquid and fire flame;
and with as little interest
in the habit of name.
        Snakily
on his toes he confronts me, his hat
like a rubber ball bobbing on
a seal's nose; while he cranes
his neck to see me in the round
with a stare like Picasso's.
Ants I can't shake off, his eyes
stalk round my chin, file through
my shirt, my trousers, bite my skin
till I am itching all over.

Immediately I begin to wriggle
pivoting, he slithers off—
as a gorilla might in clothes—
and I slump like a ransacked house
with broken windows.

For the Masked Ones

Here is a face for you, masked ones.
A real face with features on it.
The way it holds you in its glance
may startle, provoke brief disquiet;
yet there is nothing hostile here.
The forehead's active: as each thought
devises, it will subtly alter,
signal if it does not record.
Notice the eyes: enlarged, alert
one minute, deep-lidded the next.
Not glintings like glass by moonlight—
rich fires, each pupilled iris flecked
with gold. Responsive to the hour
and mood, see how they flare and fade.
Now, masked ones, look still lower.
Here is the nose. Not ruled quite straight
like yours, nor half so cardboard-stiff,
but mobile, hairy-nostrilled, pored;
of all features the most alive
once conscious, its owner expert.
The mouth, overshadowed almost,
curls just beneath. No mere dark slit
with lines for teeth, but with lips closed
or parted, flute-like, sensitive:
tight-squared in fury, roundly rolled
to hoot astonishment or kiss—
poised in this cup, the curving chin
which may lunge forward, lift with pride
or falter, scared from its position:
palpable, not blandly fitted.
A face. Not those weird things of yours,
pulped newspaper tied on with string.
All life's stigmata, lines and scars
afflict this naked, tender skin—
whatever its pigmentation,

brown, red or yellow, white or black.
Being itself it has no varnish on
which might obscure its light or dark
with aims or status, kinship, faith . . .
it needs no such apologies;
unlike you masked ones, likes to breathe
at liberty beneath all skies.
The face of neither beast nor god
nor demon: somewhat like your own
with your witch-doctor's headgear off
and superstitious rites outgrown.

The Living

This couple like two asphalt flowers
rooted securely in the sidewalk,
he with a dangling fist of messages
she mowing slowly with a pram,
defined in silhouette against the glare
grow silently yet never move:
some thread of his tobacco clouds
will always twist between the poles,
her knuckles need some hint of gold.

Before and after an explosion
such a stillness dominates all things.

JAMES K. BAXTER

High Country Weather

Alone we are born
  And die alone;
Yet see the red-gold cirrus
  Over snow-mountain shine.

Upon the upland road
  Ride easy, stranger:
Surrender to the sky
  Your heart of anger.

The Bay

On the road to the bay was a lake of rushes
Where we bathed at times and changed in the bamboos.
Now it is rather to stand and say:
How many roads we take that lead to Nowhere,
The alley overgrown, no meaning now but loss:
Not that veritable garden where everything comes easy.

And by the bay itself were cliffs with carved names
And a hut on the shore beside the maori ovens.
We raced boats from the banks of the pumice creek
Or swam in those autumnal shallows
Growing cold in amber water, riding the logs
Upstream, and waiting for the taniwha.

So now I remember the bay, and the little spiders
On driftwood, so poisonous and quick.
The carved cliffs and the great out-crying surf
With currents round the rocks and the birds rising.

A thousand times an hour is torn across
And burned for the sake of going on living.
But I remember the bay that never was
And stand like stone, and cannot turn away.

Elegy for an Unknown Soldier

There was a time when I would magnify
His ending; scatter words as if I wept
Tears not my own but man's; there was a time.
But not now so. He died of a common sickness.

Nor did any new star shine
Upon the day when he came crying out
Of fleshy darkness to a world of pain,
And waxen eyelids let the daylight enter.

So felt and tasted, found earth good enough.
Later he played with stones and wondered
If there was land beyond the dark sea rim
And where the road led out of the farthest paddock.

Awkward at school, he could not master sums.
Could you expect him then to understand
The miracle and menace of his body
That grew as mushrooms grow from dusk to dawn?

He had the weight, though, for a football scrum,
And thought it fine to listen to the cheering
And drink beer with the boys, telling them tall
Stories of girls that he had never known.

So when the War came he was glad and sorry,
But soon enlisted. Then his mother cried
A little, and his father boasted how
He'd let him go, though needed for the farm.

Likely in Egypt he would find out something
About himself, if flies and drunkenness
And deadly heat could tell him much—until
In his first battle a shell splinter caught him.

So crown him with memorial bronze among
The older dead, child of a mountainous island.
Wings of a tarnished victory shadow him
Who born of silence has burned back to silence.

Wild Bees

Often in summer, on a tarred bridge plank standing,
Or downstream between willows, a safe Ophelia drifting
In a rented boat—I had seen them come and go,
Those wild bees swift as tigers, their gauze wings a-glitter
In passionless industry, clustering black at the crevice
Of a rotten cabbage tree, where their hive was hidden low.

But never strolled too near. Till one half-cloudy evening
Of ripe January, my friends and I
Came, gloved and masked to the eyes like plundering desperadoes,
To smoke them out. Quiet beside the stagnant river
We trod wet grasses down, hearing the crickets chitter
And waiting for light to drain from the wounded sky.

Before we reached the hive their sentries saw us
And sprang invisible through the darkening air,
Stabbed, and died in stinging. The hive woke. Poisonous fuming
Of sulphur filled the hollow trunk, and crawling
Blue flame sputtered—yet still their suicidal
Live raiders dived and clung to our hands and hair.

O it was Carthage under the Roman torches,
Or loud with flames and falling timber, Troy!
A job well botched. Half of the money melted
And half the rest young grubs. Through earth-black smouldering
  ashes
And maimed bees groaning, we drew out our plunder.
Little enough their gold, and slight our joy.

Fallen then the city of instinctive wisdom.
Tragedy is written distinct and small:
A hive burned on a cool night in summer.
But loss is a precious stone to me, a nectar
Distilled in time, preaching the truth of winter
To the fallen heart that does not cease to fall.

The Morgue

Each morning when I lit the coke furnace
Unwillingly I passed the locked door,
The room where Death lived. Shadowless infection
Looked from the blind panes, and an open secret
Stained even the red flowers in the rock garden
Flesh-fingered under the sanatorium wall.

And each day the patients coming and going
From light jobs, joking below the sombre pines,
Would pass without looking, their faces leaner
As if the wintry neighbourhood of Death
Would strip the shuddering flesh from bone. They shouted,
Threw clods at one another, and passed on.

But when at length, with stiff broom and bucket,
I opened the door wide—well, there was nothing
To fear. Only the bare close concrete wall,
A slab of stone, and a wheeled canvas stretcher.
For Death had shifted house to his true home
And mansion, ruinous, of the human heart.

247

Poem in the Matukituki Valley

Some few yards from the hut the standing beeches
Let fall their dead limbs, overgrown
With feathered moss and filigree of bracken.
The rooted wood splits clean and hard
Close-grained to the driven axe, with sound of water
Sibilant falling and high-nested birds.

In winter blind with snow; but in full summer
The forest blanket sheds its cloudy pollen
And cloaks a range in undevouring fire.
Remote the land's heart: though the wild scrub cattle
Acclimatized, may learn
Shreds of her purpose, or the taloned kea.

For those who come as I do, half-aware,
Wading the swollen
Matukituki waist-high in snow water,
And stumbling where the mountains throw their dice
Of boulders huge as houses, or the smoking
Cataract flings its arrows on our path—

For us the land is matrix and destroyer
Resentful, darkly known
By sunset omens, low words heard in branches;
Or where the red deer lift their innocent heads
Snuffing the wind for danger,
And from our footfall's menace bound in terror.

Three emblems of the heart I carry folded
For charms against flood water, sliding shale:
Pale gentian, lily, and bush orchid.
The peaks too have names to suit their whiteness,
Stargazer and Moonraker,
A sailor's language and a mountaineer's.

And those who sleep in close bags fitfully
Besieged by wind in a snowline bivouac—
The carrion parrot with red underwing
Clangs on the roof by night, and daybreak brings
Raincloud on purple ranges, light reflected
Stainless from crumbling glacier, dazzling snow.

Do they not, clay in that unearthly furnace,
Endure the hermit's peace
And mindless ecstasy? Blue-lipped crevasse
And smooth rock chimney straddling—a communion
With what eludes our net—Leviathan
Stirring to ocean birth our inland waters?

Sky's purity, the altar cloth of snow
On deathly summits laid; or avalanche
That shakes the rough moraine with giant laughter;
Snowplume and whirlwind—what are these
But His flawed mirror who gave the mountain strength
And dwells in holy calm, undying freshness?

Therefore we turn, hiding our souls' dullness
From that too blinding glass: turn to the gentle
Dark of our human daydream, child and wife,
Patience of stone and soil, the lawful city
Where man may live and no wild trespass
Of what's eternal shake his grave of time.

The Homecoming

Odysseus has come home, to the gully farm
Where the macrocarpa windbreak shields a house
Heavy with time's reliques—the brown-filmed photographs
Of ghosts more real than he; the mankind-measuring arm
Of a pendulum clock; and true yet to her vows,
His mother, grief's Penelope. At the blind the sea wind laughs.

The siege more long and terrible than Troy's
Begins again. A Love demanding all,
Hypochondriacal, seadark and contentless:
This was the sour ground that nurtured a boy's
Dream of freedom; this, in Circe's hall
Drugged him; his homecoming finds this, more relentless.

She does not say, 'You have changed'; nor could she imagine any
Otherwise to the quiet maelstrom spinning
In the circle of their days. Still she would wish to carry
Him folded within her, shut from the wild and many
Voices of life's combat, in the cage of beginning;
She counts it natural that he should never marry.

She will cook his meals; complain of the south weather
That wrings her joints. And he—rebels; and yields
To the old covenant—calms the bleating
Ewe in birth travail. The smell of saddle leather
His sacrament; or the sale day drink; yet hears beyond sparse
    fields
On reef and cave the sea's hexameter beating.

Lament for Barney Flanagan

Licensee of the Hesperus Hotel

Flanagan got up on a Saturday morning,
Pulled on his pants while the coffee was warming;
He didn't remember the doctor's warning,
    'Your heart's too big, Mr. Flanagan.'

Barney Flanagan, sprung like a frog
From a wet root in an Irish bog—
May his soul escape from the tooth of the dog!
    God have mercy on Flanagan.

Barney Flanagan R.I.P.
Rode to his grave on Hennessey's
Like a bottle-cork boat in the Irish Sea.
  The bell-boy rings for Flanagan.

Barney Flanagan, ripe for a coffin,
Eighteen stone and brandy-rotten,
Patted the housemaid's velvet bottom—
  'Oh, is it you, Mr. Flanagan?'

The sky was bright as a new milk token.
Bill the Bookie and Shellshock Hogan
Waited outside for the pub to open—
  'Good day, Mr. Flanagan.'

At noon he was drinking in the lounge bar corner
With a sergeant of police and a racehorse owner
When the Angel of Death looked over his shoulder—
  'Could you spare a moment, Flanagan?'

Oh the deck was cut; the bets were laid;
But the very last card that Barney played
Was the Deadman's Trump, the bullet of Spades—
  'Would you like more air, Mr. Flanagan?'

The priest came running but the priest came late
For Barney was banging at the Pearly Gate.
St. Peter said, 'Quiet! You'll have to wait
  For a hundred masses, Flanagan.'

The regular boys and the loud accountants
Left their nips and their seven-ounces
As chickens fly when the buzzard pounces—
  'Have you heard about old Flanagan?'

Cold in the parlour Flanagan lay
Like a bride at the end of her marriage day.
The Waterside Workers' Band will play
  A brass good-bye to Flanagan.

While publicans drink their profits still,
While lawyers flock to be in at the kill,
While Aussie barmen milk the till
   We will remember Flanagan.

For Barney had a send-off and no mistake.
He died like a man for his country's sake;
And the Governor-General came to his wake.
   Drink again to Flanagan!

Despise not, O Lord, the work of Thine own hands
And let light perpetual shine upon him.

My Love Late Walking

My love late walking in the rain's white aisles
I break words for, though many tongues
Of night deride and the moon's boneyard smile

Cuts to the quick our newborn sprig of song.
See and believe, my love, the late yield
Of bright grain, the sparks of harvest wrung

From difficult joy. My heart is an open field.
There you may stray wide or stand at home
Nor dread the giant's bone and broken shield

Or any tendril locked on a thunder stone,
Nor fear, in the forked grain, my hawk who flies
Down to your feathered sleep alone

Striding blood coloured on a wind of sighs.
Let him at the heart of your true dream move,
My love, in the lairs of hope behind your eyes.

I sing, to the rain's harp, of light renewed,
The black tares broken, fresh the phoenix light
I lost among time's rags and burning tombs.

My love walks long in harvest aisles tonight.

Crossing Cook Strait

The night was clear, sea calm; I came on deck
To stretch my legs, find perhaps
Gossip, a girl in green slacks at the rail
Or just the logline feathering a dumb wake.

The ship swung in the elbow of the Strait.
'Dolphins!' I cried—'let the true sad Venus
Rise riding her shoals, teach me at once to wonder
And wander at ease, be glad and never regret.'

But night increased under the signal stars.
In the dark bows, facing the flat sea,
Stood one I had not expected, yet knew without surprise
As the Janus made formidable by loveless years.

His coat military; his gesture mild—
'Well met,' he said, 'on the terrestrial journey
From chaos into light—what light it is
Contains our peril and purpose, history has not revealed.'

'Sirs—' I began. He spoke with words of steel—
'I am Seddon and Savage, the socialist father.
You have known me only in my mask of Dionysus
Amputated in bar rooms, dismembered among wheels.

'I woke in my civil tomb hearing a shout
For bread and justice. It was not here.
That sound came thinly over the waves from China;
Stones piled on my grave had all but shut it out.

'I walked forth gladly to find the angry poor
Who are my nation; discovered instead
The glutton seagulls squabbling over crusts
And policies made and broken behind locked doors.

'I have watched the poets also at their trade.
I have seen them burning with a wormwood brilliance.
Love was the one thing lacking on their page,
The crushed herb of grief at another's pain.

'Your civil calm breeds inward poverty
That chafes for change. The ghost of Adam
Gibbering demoniac in drawing-rooms
Will drink down hemlock with his sugared tea.

'You feed your paupers concrete. They work well,
Ask for no second meal, vote, pay tribute
Of silence on Anzac Day in the pub urinal;
Expose death only by a mushroom smell.

'My counsel was naïve. Anger is bread
To the poor, their guns more accurate than justice,
Because their love has not decayed to a wintry fungus
And hope to the wish for power among the dead.

'In Kaitangata the miner's falling sweat
Wakes in the coal seam fossil flowers.
The clerk puts down his pen and takes his coat;
He will not be back today or the next day either.'

With an ambiguous salute he left me.
The ship moved into a stronger sea
Bludgeoned alive by the rough mystery
Of love in the running straits of history.

Green Figs at Table

'To eat a green fig, my dear,
Torn from the belly of unreason,
Honey white or brown when you open it,
The female parts, a story, or a poem—'
  'Perhaps.'

'The taste sticks in one's mouth. Even now
Barometer wounds begin to throb, simply
Because you are a woman, woman in her rubbed flesh
Dressed for carnage—' 'I thought there was
  A better name for it.'

'Action. Society as undertaker
Measures us for coffins, plugs up the orifices
By which pleasure might enter or pity escape.
Mothers admire the handsome corpse
  That cost so little

'To be tidied. They cover the rope mark on the throat.'
'You were talking of figs—' 'Yes, figs.
I would like to be, at length, Odysseus lounging
With loaf and wine-cup in the shade
  Of his daughter the bent olive,

'But I too roast in the brass bull
Of conscience, remembering at this autumn table
Women ganched in cupboards of the mind or
Geometrical on the black glaze of an urn—'
  'I burn in waiting

'For the sea to rise or the god to descend
And hear, in coffee shops, the mill of gossip turning.'
'Blood runs from my nail into the soya dish;
Oil boats rust, chained at darkened wharves.
  One movement could shake

'Us free, I think—' 'One should not say too much.
Enter, without knocking, the door of the fig.'

At Akitio

Consider this barbarian coast,
Traveller, you who have lost
Lover or friend. It has never made
Anything out of anything.
Drink at these bitter springs.

Fishing at river mouth, a woman
Uses the sea-drilled stone her mother used
For sinker, as big kahawai come,
As tides press upward to time's source.
This coast is shelter to the shearing gangs
Who burn dead matai in their kitchen.

Squirearch, straight-backed rider, built
An ethos of the leisured life,
Lawn, antlered hall and billiard room,
Glass candelabra brought from Paris,
The homestead foundered among fields.
Unhorsed they sleep.

A girl with a necklace of mako teeth
They dug from a sandcliff facing south,
Axe and broken needle.
Stay good under slab and cross
Thin bones of children burnt by cholera,
Made tidy by the last strict nurse.
As tributary of a greater stream
Your single grief enlarges now
The voice of night in kumara gardens,
Prayer of the bush pigeon.

One drowned at the cattle crossing,
One tossed and kicked by a bucking horse—
Who died without confession, wanting

No wafer in their teeth—
Does the toi-toi plume their altar?
Are they held safe in the sea's grail?

This gullied mounded earth, tonned
With silence, and the sun's gaze
On a choir of breakers, has outgrown
The pain of love. Drink,
Traveller, at these pure springs.

Remember, though, the early strength
Of bull-voiced water when the boom broke
And eels clung to the banks, logs
Plunged and pierced the river hymen.
Remember iron-coloured skulls
Of cattle thrown to the crab's crypt,
Driftwood piled by river flood
On the long beach, battered limb
And loin where the red-backed spider breeds,
By a halcyon sea the shapes of man,
Emblems of our short fever.

Pluck then from ledges of the sea
Crayfish for the sack. Not now but later
Think what you were born for. Drink,
Child, at the springs of sleep.

Perseus

Leaving them, children of the Sun, to their perpetual
Unwearying dance about the ancient Tree,
Perseus flew east, the bird-winged sandals beating
Smooth and monotonous; sauntered above
Fens peopled by the placid watersnake,
Flamingo, crocodile—

And those unfallen creatures, joyful in
Their maze of waters, watched; with reedy voices
Praised the oncoming hero; cried
And coupled in his path. But he felt only
Scorching his shoulders, the shield, Athene's love-
gift—and the first
Wind of foreboding blow from Medusa's home.

So entered the stone kingdom where no life
Startled, but brackish water fell
Like tears from solitary beds
Of sphagnum moss, or spray from cataracts
Sprinkled the grey-belled orchid, feathered grass
And spider's coverlet.

Till by the final cleft precipitous
At a blind gorge's end he lighted, stood,
Unslung the heavy shield, drew breath, and waited
As the bright hornet waits and quivers
Hearing within her den the poisonous rustle
And mew, for battle angry, of tarantula.

Fair smote her face upon the burning shield,
Medusa, image of the soul's despair,
Snake-garlanded, child of derisive Chaos
And hateful Night, whom no man may
Look on and live. In horror, pity, loathing,
Perseus looked long, lifted his sword, and struck.

Then empty was the cave. A vulture's taloned body
Headless and huddled, a woman's marble face
With snakes for hair—and in the wide
Thoroughfares of the sky no hint of cloudy fury
Or clanging dread, as homeward he
Trod, the pouched Despair at his girdle hanging,

258

To earth, Andromeda, the palace garden
His parents bickered in, plainsong of harvest—
To the lawgiver's boredom, rendering
(The task accomplished) back to benignant Hermes
And holy Athene goods not his own, the borrowed
Sandals of courage and the shield of art.

Howrah Bridge

to my wife

Taller than the stair of Qtub Minar
These iron beams oppress the eagle's town.
Bare heels will dint them slowly.
And swollen Gunga's muscles move
Beneath, with freight of garbage,
Oar and sail, the loot of many lives.

In the unsleeping night my thoughts
Are millet falling from an iron pan,
While you, my dear, in Delhi lying down
Enter the same room by another door.
The rupee god has trampled here;
The poor implore a Marxist cage.
Dragon seed, the huddled bundles lying
In doorways have perhaps one chilli,
A handful of ground maize.
King Famine rules. Tout and owl-eyed whore
Whose talons pluck and stain the sleeve,
Angels of judgement, husk the soul
Till pity, pity only stays.

Out of my wounds they have made stars:
Each is an eye that looks on you.

On the Death of Her Body

It is a thought breaking the granite heart
Time has given me, that my one treasure,
Your limbs, those passion-vines, that bamboo body

Should age and slacken, rot
Some day in a ghastly clay-stopped hole.
They led me to the mountains beyond pleasure

Where each is not gross body or blank soul
But a strong harp the wind of genesis
Makes music in, such resonant music

That I was Adam, loosened by your kiss
From time's hard bond, and you,
My love, in the world's first summer stood

Plucking the flowers of the abyss.

Election 1960

Hot sun. Lizards frolic
Fly-catching on the black ash

That was green rubbish. Tiny dragons,
They dodge among the burnt broom stems

As if the earth belonged to them
Without condition. In the polling booths

A democratic people have elected
King Log, King Stork, King Log, King Stork again.

Because I like a wide and silent pond
I voted Log. That party was defeated.

Now frogs will dive and scuttle to avoid
That poking idiot bill, the iron gullet:

Delinquent frogs! Stork is an active King,
A bird of principle, benevolent,

And Log is Log, an old time-serving post
Hacked from a totara when the land was young.

Ballad of Calvary Street

On Calvary Street are trellises
Where bright as blood the roses bloom,
And gnomes like pagan fetishes
Hang their hats on an empty tomb
Where two old souls go slowly mad,
National Mum and Labour Dad.

Each Saturday when full of smiles
The children come to pay their due,
Mum takes down the family files
And cover to cover she thumbs them through,
Poor Len before he went away
And Mabel on her wedding day.

The meal-brown scones display her knack,
Her polished oven spits with rage,
While in Grunt Grotto at the back
Dad sits and reads the Sporting Page,
Then ambles out in boots of lead
To weed around the parsnip bed.

A giant parsnip sparks his eye,
Majestic as the Tree of Life:
He washes it and rubs it dry

And takes it in to his old wife—
'Look Laura, would that be a fit?
The bastard has a flange on it!'

When both were young she would have laughed,
A goddess in her tartan skirt,
But wisdom, age and mothercraft
Have rubbed it home that men like dirt:
Five children and a fallen womb,
A golden crown beyond the tomb.

Nearer the bone, sin is sin,
And women bear the cross of woe,
And that affair with Mrs. Flynn
(It happened thirty years ago)
Though never mentioned, means that he
Will get no sugar in his tea.

The afternoon goes by, goes by,
The angels harp above a cloud,
A son-in-law with spotted tie
And daughter Alice fat and loud
Discuss the virtues of insurance
And stuff their tripes with trained endurance.

Flood-waters hurl upon the dyke
And Dad himself can go to town,
For little Charlie on his trike
Has ploughed another iris down.
His parents rise to chain the beast,
Brush off the last crumbs of their lovefeast.

And so these two old fools are left,
A rosy pair in evening light,
To question Heaven's dubious gift,
To hag and grumble, growl and fight:
The love they kill won't let them rest,
Two birds that peck in one fouled nest.

Why hammer nails? Why give no change?
Habit, habit clogs them dumb.
The Sacred Heart above the range
Will bleed and burn till Kingdom Come,
But Yin and Yang won't ever meet
In Calvary Street, in Calvary Street.

from *Pig Island Letters*

2

From an old house shaded with macrocarpas
Rises my malady.
Love is not valued much in Pig Island
Though we admire its walking parody,

That brisk gaunt woman in the kitchen
Feeding the coal range, sullen
To all strangers, lest one should be
Her antique horn-red Satan.

Her man, much baffled, grousing in the pub,
Discusses sales
Of yearling lambs, the timber in a tree
Thrown down by autumn gales,

Her daughter, reading in her room
A catalogue of dresses,
Can drive a tractor, goes to Training College,
Will vote on the side of the Bosses,

Her son is moodier, has seen
An angel with a sword
Standing above the clump of old man manuka
Just waiting for the word

To overturn the cities and the rivers
And split the house like a rotten totara log.
Quite unconcerned he sets his traps for possums
And whistles to his dog.

The man who talks to the masters of Pig Island
About the love they dread
Plaits ropes of sand, yet I was born among them
And will lie some day with their dead.

The Beach House

The wind outside this beach house
Shaking the veranda rail
Has the weight of the sky behind its blows,
A violence stronger than the fable

Of life and art. Sitting alone
Late at the plywood table,
I have become a salt-scoured bone
Tumbling in the drifted rubble,

And you, my love, sleep under quilts within
The square bunk-room. When I was young
(Hot words and brandy on my tongue)
Only the grip of breast, mouth, loin,

Could ward off the incubus
Of night's rage. Now I let
The waters grind me, knowing well that the sweet
Daybreak behind your eyes

Will not be struck dead by any wind,
And we will walk on the shore
A day older, while the yoked waves thunder,
As if the storm were a dream. Sleep sound.

At Taieri Mouth

Flax-pods unload their pollen
Above the steel-bright cauldron

Of Taieri, the old water-dragon
Sliding out from a stone gullet

Below the Maori-ground. Scrub horses
Come down at night to smash the fences

Of the whaler's children. Trypots have rusted
Leaving the oil of anger in the blood

Of those who live in two-roomed houses
Mending nets or watching from a window

The great south sky fill up with curdled snow.
Their cows eat kelp along the beaches.

The purple sailor drowned in thighboots
Drifting where the currents go

Cannot see the flame some girl has lighted
In a glass chimney, but in five days' time

With bladder-weed around his throat
Will ride the drunken breakers in.

The Lion Skin

The old man with a yellow flower on his coat
Came to my office, climbing twenty-eight steps,
With a strong smell of death about his person
From the caves of the underworld.
The receptionist was troubled by his breath
Understandably.

                Not every morning tea break
Does Baron Saturday visit his parishioners
Walking stiffly, strutting almost,
With a cigar in his teeth—she might have remembered
Lying awake as if nailed by a spear
Two nights ago, with the void of her life
Glassed in a dark window—but suitably enough
She preferred to forget it.

                I welcomed him
And poured him a glass of cherry brandy,
Talked with him for half an hour or so,
Having need of his strength, the skin of a dead lion,
In the town whose ladders are made of coffin wood.

The flower on his coat blazed like a dark sun.

PAT WILSON

The Anchorage

Fifteen or twenty feet below,
The little fish come creeping round the anchor chain.
I could not have it quieter now,
Not anywhere, nor could there be less movement
Anywhere at all than here.

The bay moves on into night.
The shadows come to watch and wait in every hollow
Till they have gathered-in all.
But moon comes over the rocks; she lights the little fall
And rise and fall at the beach.

Deep water, deep bay
So still and calm for one whole night in the south-east
That day has never come,
And I am still upon my knees out on the stern,
And you and I still watch
Down twenty, thirty feet below.

The Farewell

And so, one day when the tide was away out,
The gulls there dancing along the edge of the sea,
We walked across the sand, down to the boat
And began again—she to protest and appeal,
I to refuse, looking aside, and then turning
And smiling . . .

           for it was not as if I had
Whatever it was that she asked, but who could persuade
        her
Of that? nor was it true that I could pretend

For ever . . .

          and all the gulls there, crying and playing,
Hunting, and all the reds and browns and yellows
Of late afternoon, and the last tints of the blue
Going out with the tide, and the boat drawn up there fast
Becoming high and dry on the sand as we talked.

Cuvier Light

Perennial fluctuation,
Interior lift of the sea,
Mist or a light rain, and silence—

Suppose our breathing is this movement,
This mist, our wishes coming back to us,
The rain, some forgiveness of our rashness,
The night, all that is against us—

Land all along one side,
One lamp turned low in the cabin,
Two lights to sea and then great Cuvier,

Admirable light!
Swinging, like a discus
On the arm of its taut brilliant beam,
The whole massed weight of the night!

The Tree

The day the big tree went
There came two rather seedy-looking men
Full of mysteries of their craft.
They spoke loudly yet confidentially to each other,
Nodded to me and my brother,
Said good morning to my brother's wife,
Cleared away all the little children of the neighbourhood,
And addressed themselves
To their big, supple saw.

Two or three hours later under the tree
They were still only half-way through.
The cut had a tell-tale concave scoop
Where each had been pulling down at the end of his stroke.
There was much previous talk of wedges,
Much arranging of ropes,
Calculation of angles,
And my brother and I were taking turns at the saw.

And so we all got friendly there with each other,
Putting the mysteries away
Under the great macrocarpa tree.
And when it started to lift and heave
And when the earth shook and the great sigh went up
As it fell and settled,
Then all the birds came flying out in a cloud
And all the children flew in with shouts and cries
And started a battle with the cones
And made their huts and houses in the fir.

The Precious Pearl

The oyster shuts his gates to form the pearl.
He knows he has a saviour caught within him,
Poor fool, old oyster. And it works against him,
An irritant that's locked within his shell,
A single-mindedness that thins his heart,
Turns it to narrowheartedness. Yet he,
Poor fool, poor oyster, used to love the sea
In all its many forms, to every part
Open with tranquil, unassuming jaws.
Then that foul irritant was driven in,
And snap! the wounded tongue cherished its sin
Until at last by hard, immobile laws
    A shining, perfect pebble made from wrong—
    A perfect grievance—rolled from off the tongue.

CHARLES DOYLE

Empirical History

Why should a man think because the heart is vulnerable
that he can beat the drum, make incantation
out of the names of rivers, the green rhythm of love,
birds of flamed plumage in a sky of oil?

Why should I be the one whose crucible
yields up the potent meaning of resurrection
or mouths the words of the orator that move
rough hands to the weeping faces, sway the will?

In all dew mornings the scuttling spiders' fingers
net up the wet, high hedges, glacial with diamonds;
and in the darkness hands move with their secret praise,
gentle but still demanding whose is the poem now?

O surely where the uncertain, poised hands linger
there is beauty there and a fire and wonder beyond
label; but there is also dread, pain, war, voices, the way
silence swings through that vast and empty house.

Again the rose opens an unhealed wound and no sounds
mean 'rose' more than any other; nor is any white thing
that one can speak of as white as the mortal snow
melting in death's cauldron, drowning, flooding the flames.

No, though the heart is vulnerable the wounds
are their own lost voices; only they can sing
what they feel. Whoever made us made it so
we have no more than an eye and a flair for names.

Starlings and History

It is again time when sleek and glossy starlings
Invade the lawn in their gentlemanly lemon
And black, comical shakos of their beaks
Thrust forward. Under their clamorous murmurations
      Summer has babbled in.

Oblivious, noisy creatures, they have heralded or
Said farewell to all the seasons of all my life.
I, too, have seen them on a grey slate roof
Or commuting into trees alive with leaf,
      Or dead on the dark road.

And now, now only I mouth to myself and the glass,
'These are alive, too. Everything lives and moves,
Grows and has meaning.' I recall as I grope for meaning
How once, a boy in the slums, I loved those roofs'
      Grey slate in winter sky;

Brick houses underneath, dark-honeycombed
With little rooms; brass bedsteads, pedestals
Of mottled marble, cracked linoleum;
In the yard a shower of orange blossom petals,
      Path of powdery bricks;

Those Friday nights I listened to the one-man band,
Bass drum and barrel organ by the painted house
On the corner, where the old lady gave us sugar;
How for supper we always opened a tin of sardines,
      Were allowed to stay up late.

Such things are history or happiness,
The quarrel with ourselves, self-renewal
Which Amiel demands of the living soul.
Man must embrace all being, both the cruel
      And, what hurts more, the gentle.

Our corner of time and place, of muted sufferings,
Loud enjoyments, decked in lewd, banal
Catchphrases, snapshots, comics and popular songs,
Though it must be, is all that we are, final
          Measure of us and all things,

Man's meaning and the world's. In the dead life of my life
I hear children cry out among the bracken,
The drowned one quiet, her desolate bucket and spade
Unkempt on the shore of our breathing, her parents stricken
          To another death on the pier.

I see priests in their cassocks and the wild honey
On the refectory table when mine was a golden eye;
Later the creaking hawser, eyes of shorelights
Open, I cast adrift on totalitarian sea
          To discover another self.

From all the seas of my selves I wake and wonder
When the torture of knowing shakes my soul from its torpor,
Knowing that all must end in the unknown voyage
Out of the world of bricks and kicking and the lure
          And deviltry of love.

Every eclectic marvellous detail,
Coarse Wiltshire stone under the caring hand,
Giant kauris aching upon the eye, every kind of love,
Even pity and ceremony must end
          Between the quiet poles.

Now I turn, find it is winter. Dreary birds
Make the grey air untidy, their rough-gutted screech
A hubbub that disturbs me. I suddenly know that all worlds
Are chequered and drab like these, that promise of rich
          Permanent summer is false.

Still there are seasons, summers, migrations,
Flowerings and rebirths. Even the hooded candles
Will gleam upon the reviving ceremonial.
Living and dying seem endless; nothing is endless.
One does not die for ever.

Being Here (or Anywhere)

So much behind the bald phrase. One might say
To be assigned particular location
Means no more than it states, banally, yet
Take whichever word you will you get

Untold qualifications. To be in being may
Not need another's voice to tabulate
What 'is' describes, but 'is' itself assumes
A place in time, in the sun. You can locate

Yourself by the mere assumption, but cannot
Communicate without the 'here' and 'there'.
Aim or stability, simple sufferance, needs
Other description. Adjectives dispel

Both emptiness and immediacy, remain
Refinements, limits. Pain, holiness
Are ours in the instance. We are shut in
By categories, labels, who must not be less

Than what we are, or where. Sophistication
Merely adds other questions. Our joy, fear,
Are told in tenses. World's love lies
In the word you find to answer the searching, 'Where?'

Duel in the Camellias

(after Tristan Corbière)

I've seen the sun sword-slashing hard
　　Against the blossom. I've seen two swords of sun,
Two swords making mock parries, comic thrusts;
　　Watching them sparkle, some blackbirds shadow-hidden.

The arranged sleeve of a swordsman's linen blouse,
　　So seemed to me the giant white camellia;
Another flower, pink, poised on the branch,
　　Pink as can be . . . then flashed a rapier.

Red . . . It's true! . . . They are cutting each other's throats—
A white camellia—there—the throat of Christ . . .
A camellia's yellow—here—bedraggled, crushed . . .

Dead love, fallen from my buttonhole.
—For me, an open wound and a spring flower,
Living camellia, with an aplomb of blood!

Messages for Herod

Saved by his foreign tongue, one king
Whom Herod had asked to report back
Kept his counsel and travelled home
By a different track.

'Imagination, that's the place,'
The second one told Herod,
'Where the kid's king, so his mum says.'
'A desert! Who needs it!' Herod cried.

But a smashed ikon the third brought
Set Herod's soldiers slaughtering,
For the kid had destroyed a cash slogan:
'Queen Street: Centre of Everything'.

OWEN LEEMING

End of Season

Between night and this morning's dawn, purple
Over sea-view villas, pine-needle hills,
   There has been a shadowy withdrawal.
Eyelids have closed, and stayed that way, leaving the light
To jingle its gold, to crash and to hammer, outside.

Dust feels dustier, light harsher, and sea more solemn,
In this sudden First of October stillness.

All humans seem somehow survivors, even humans
Who belong with this place. Boatmen in sweaters,
   Left to themselves,
Natter secretly under the mole, suspecting bad weather,
While their bright boats chop uneasily on their chains.
In town, it is entirely secret, stowed away, hot and speechless.
Closed, shuttered are the pensions. Closed the shops which sold
   Aqualungs, frogfeet, spears.

Was there a warning of disaster, some imminent catastrophe,
   last night
To sweep those bronzed boys, those bleached girls away?
They and their voices might never have been here.
   The place has an air
Of waiting for earthquake, or for plague, or a landing from Mars.

Only on the beach an Englishman, with white knees,
Reading Euripides, a boy lifting off doors
   From bathing sheds,
A few pedal-boats that look like cast-up bones,
And a line of footprints, single, already being washed away.

At four in the afternoon, there are clouds.
On the point, olives and pines bristle, sigh.
   The Englishman goes inside.

A blackness comes into the sea. Under the mole,
Boatmen nod to one another wisely. Tomorrow, as they foresaw,
  Cold and spray will ratify
  What convention did today.

The Priests of Serrabonne

I

For three sodden miles,
The engine howls, scaling a winding stair
Of mud, hauling me up the rugged grade
  Where the past and my past are laid.
Below are olive-trees, veils of rain, tiles
  Of the vanishing cottage where
  The caretaker spits among piles

Of onions, postcards, rope.
Brown slime and stones give off a poisonous chill
'You're not wanted' feel. The past of sheep
  And villages is fast asleep.
I make this road a trail, where neophytes grope
  To their grave, or God's will
  As they would say, whose slope

Carries them apart, each face
Sour with sweat as they trudge the world behind.
I'm re-creating. For history's mild or savage men
  I see today's brethren,
Trappist and Carmelite, filling their empty space;
  And free my apostate mind
  From veracity's saving grace.

277

Braving the uncivil air,
I come at last to Serrabonne. It transfixes me—
An outline which knifes from mist, such scorn in stone,
 A tower so harshly hewn,
I know I can never forget, with its three square
  Apertures up high, three
  Blanks whose bleak stare

  Dissuades approach. Those eyes
And socket nose, gable, the verticals' hard
Uncompromise, that is the logic of monastic rule,
 Its limit at least, in cruel
Line. Hills, endless, boring, rise
  Like sea-swell. In them is barred
  The priory, whose force supplies

  Resisting force in me.
Grown over with blue-black scrub, scarred by snow,
Scoured by rain, this landscape prompts extreme
 Inhabiting. Its figures seem
Amalgamates of all devotion to that cause. In scree,
  Hardship; snow, the glow
  Of flagellated flesh; monotony

  Of hills, the regular rote-led
Lives. Disputing the cause, I can still admire
The gritty saints who've built upon this ground,
 The guts of will that bound
Them to self-death during life. Their tower, a head
  Without humour or desire,
  Glares across the lead

  Coloured, lachrymose skies
Its mission to crush the senses while, here below,
The oblong priory church, a fortress barn,
 Looks imitatively stern,

Repeating in its way the tower's command—to despise
      The world's lures. I go
      To its door. The keyhole cries

      As the corroded foot-long key
Voluptuously inches in. I wonder if they thought
Of that, the monks? It turns with a rusty crash.
      From the creaking door, a gash
Of daylight widens in the dark. Enough to see,
      Be staggered by, a wrought,
      A shadow-fragile filigree

      Of marble, carved in pink!
Riotously carved at that. Vines and palms,
Little bent men, thin pillars alive
      With pattern, defiantly survive
In veined fleshy stone. What can one think?
      Is this rostrum up in arms
      Against the tower, or a link

      With it? Oasis of art
In Serrabonne's Lenten desert, I find
It dares condone the human. Then, looking through
      Its pillars to the altar renews
At once the tower's dominion. Excepting a dart
      Of light thinly outlined
      By an embrasure, no aids start

      From gloom to further the least
Emollient thoughts. A grey threshold, worn
Hollow by midnight sandals, leads to a stark
      Nave, and on through dark
To an altar of rock that less recalls the Feast
      In the Upper Room than a horn
      Or obsidian knife, a beast

Bleating before its blood
Is let. Tower, rostrum, and altar, are these
The three faces of religion, Christianity above all?
        In the thick darkness, tall
Cowled presences gather, their footfalls thud
        To their places, they bend their knees,
        Sing Tenebrae without a sound.

III

Re-creating still. But this
Impinges, spells a history mine not theirs.
These priests are formed on mine: I was taught
        By priests; less strict, but thought
In this dark shell imposes essence—the kiss
        Of celebrant on altar bears
        The weight of my religious

Past. Contemplatives, nuns,
Brothers, wearers of habits, rattlers of beads,
Office chanters, watchers of Mass behind screens,
        'Brides of Christ' . . . it means
Another Order now. Their vow of silence
        Is made to silence, and leads
        To ending, curt as guns,

Gas or poleaxe. They kill
Their life and gain a double death; they pray
To space and energy, a witless God. At Serrabonne,
        Where the light has nearly gone,
Augustinians prayed and preached, their will
        Subserving God's, no day
        Their own. And are there still.

Above the altar, the slit
Of natural light fades and so does hope
Of concord. Another wooden doorway leads
    Outside again, with weeds
Growing under, to a chopped-off cloister, a bit
    Of arch across a slope
    That darkens like the Pit.

The hard tower stands,
An iron-willed Superior, against the cloud.
Even with faith, I jibbed against monastic rule.
    Living at boarding school,
With daily Mass, silence in dorm, our hands
    Knobbed with frost, I bowed
    Uncertainly to all demands

To conquer private urge.
Impurity, meaning sex, and intellectual pride
Were drummed in as deadliest sins. And yet
    It was not the toughness set
Me riddles, discipline, but aiming to purge
    Oneself of self. Beside
    The fierce ones, monks who scourge

Their backs with little whips,
Our practice was pale enough. No less real.
'Not my will,' we prayed, 'but Thine be done.'
    Human nature was the one
Equation for sin. I forced my sprouting lips
    To shape what I could not feel:
    That flesh was bad. Perhaps

I do my teachers wrong—
My final year I won the golden cross
For Doctrine, if that counts. In Doctrine class
    We sometimes tried to pass
The 'asses' bridge' on life enclosed. The long
    Debate would run. 'They're a loss
    To the militant Church. To be strong,

It needs these mystics here
In the world, active for Christ.' A stock reply
Was dealt: 'By sanctity and prayer they store up grace,
      Provide atonement, which pays
In part the debt of sin.' 'Sanctity,' I fear,
      Meant self-rejection; as if high
      In heaven God, austere

      Accountant, drew up files
Of good and bad and entered these supreme
Oblations from monks and nuns against impurity and pride.
      All I heard implied
This crude belief. I then believed.
                    The miles
      Of hills have settled, dream
      Extended, into piles

      Of time, the centuries they hold.
I think of priests who cowed me—tall soutaned
Caners who vaunted their humility, their wall
      Of pride hung with a small
Black cross. They are singing now, controlled
      In me. Why do they hand
      Away their vitals, mould

      Themselves to the nothing which is God?
Roughly, I think, insurance: against despair,
The deepest fear; against the yoke of choice,
      Their nagging inward voice;
Against the arduousness of love. For reward, they plod
      Securely, conforming in rare
      Suburban bliss. The rod

      Is always there to make
Their bodies knuckle down. For some, this too
Insures: pain now, not after. So I explain
      What I abhor, the vain

Denaturing of life. At Serrabonne, they take
    Senses, feelings, true
    Desires, burn at the stake

    And leave an anti-man.
From this ledge where monks have shuffled, I look out on
  France,
I, condemning, admiring, fearing them; because
    I no longer believe there was,
Is, or shall be, the God who approved their plan
    Of suicide. I stake my chance
    On the fading world I scan.

IV

    A thousand years ago,
As now, the Church had money, jobs and land,
Affording comfort with salvation. Yet she built
    Her convents, easing guilt
By hiring cells to saints, the ones who go
    Without, who crave to withstand
    Their nature. Rent would flow

    In kind: an aureole of grace
On the plaster Body of Christ, a pure tower,
Cut like logic, above this scrubby world.
    Their lives are whole, curled
Without a join about their core. My case
    Denies this core, its power
    Not God but hate. I praise

    The wholeness though. With hate
Of self as premise, they build the tower their life
Around and over in flawless logic. Art
    And love have a human heart,
Cherish both self and world, the proper state,
    A greater whole. God's knife
    Cuts cold at me, but cuts too late.

V

Night thickens and rain
Spatters on the stone. I turn through the door. A grey
Pencil marks the altar—altar of sacrifice,
      Mass and men, twice
Over, body and blood. Its horizontals stain
      The dark darker where they pray,
      Those hooded presences of my brain.

      Through the night they will pray
And chant their Office, matins and mass, the priests
Of my mind, exalting their release from flesh,
      The fleshly chains that enmesh
A sinning world. I grope to the blur of day
      And leave them at their feasts
      Of conquest. So I stray

      To that splendour of chiselled pink
Which warmed me before with its carnal fire. It seems
Now a forest of young trees, rich and dense,
      Embossed like bark with the intense
Humanness of art. My eyes prickle. I think
      More softly. The sculptors' dreams
      Survive; my ascetics shrink

      In a cone of sound. To relate
This rostrum to tower and altar would be, I suppose,
To understand the whole of man. Too much for me.
      But it exists, indisputably,
A wild effusion in the chaste rigour of straight
      Barren surfaces, rose
      Amidst the grey. It is late,

      I must leave, dragging the door
Shut, crash, withdrawing the key inch
By inch, then waiting for quiet to settle. The sky
      Is sullen purple as I,

Holding the key, stand at the lintel. Before
     I leave, I want to clinch
     The union, trying once more

     To bond the lovers of sense,
Illuminators, carvers, with the haters of sense who froze
And whipped and silenced. All for God. All
     For nothing . . . man cannot maul
His nature to complete abstraction! So, instead of tense
     Antithesis, art *might* pose
     With logic without offence.

     Rough guessing that it fits,
I squelch across the grass and pass a very small
Peach tree which flinches in the rain. Planted by man,
     Frail thing, it only can
In this whole wilderness portray those sandalled misfits
     In any human way. For all
     Their praying, they have some bits

     Of gravelly garden in which
They can potter and watch their seeds come up. Yes, again
I'm re-creating, with no cause now except a tree.
     The tower, as I look behind me,
Withers my attempt at contact. Letting in the clutch,
     I escape from its gaunt disdain.
     Would a postcard cost too much?

C. K. STEAD

Carpe Diem

Since Juliet's on ice, and Joan
Staked her chips on a high throne—

Sing a waste of dreams that are
Caressing, moist, familiar:

A thousand maidens offering
Their heads to have a poet sing;

Hard-drinking beaches laced with sun,
The torn wave where torn ships run

To wine and whitewashed bungalows.
This summer sing what winter knows:

Love keeps a cuckoo in its clock,
And death's the hammer makes the stroke.

Pictures in a Gallery Undersea

I

Binnorie, O Binnorie

In Ladbroke Square the light on waxen branches—
The orange light through two veined leaves
Tenacious in frost.
        Upstairs, she lit the gas,
And drew bright curtains on the whitened eaves,
And said (her hand above the slowly turning disc)
'I shall never go back'.

Mozart in the delicate air
Slid from her glass, beat vainly against the cushions,
Then took off gladly across the deserted Square.
'You too must stay' (loosening her sun-bleached hair)
'You more than I—you will defeat their fashions.'

Invisible fins guided her to my chair.

Pictures in a gallery undersea
Were turned facing the wall, and the corridors were endless;
But in the marine distance, floating always beyond me,
A girl played Mozart on her sun-bleached hair.

So that wherever I walked on that long haul, midnight to dawn,
Stones of a sunken city woke, and passed the word,
And slept behind me; but the notes were gone,
Vanished like bubbles up through the watery air
Of London, nor would again be heard.

II

Où tant de marbre est tremblant sur tant d'ombres

On steps of the British Museum the snow falls,
The snow falls on Bloomsbury, on Soho, on all
Cradled in the great cup of London.
On all the lions and literary men of London
Heaping in gutters, running away in drains
The falling snow, the city falling.

Snow behind iron railings, drifts, collects,
Collects like coins in the corners of Nelson's hat
(Newbolt from a window in the Admiralty shouting
'Umbrellas for Nelson' and waving a sheaf of odes)
And down the long avenue.

There through her aquid glass
Circumambient Regina, turning slowly from the pane,
Is seen imperiously to mouth 'Albert, my dear,
How do we pronounce *Waitangi*?'
                              And snow descends.

There I met my grandfather, young and bearded,
With thick Scandinavian accent, who asked me
Directions to the dock; and later departed,
Bearing me with him in his northern potency
South.
        South. Earth's nether side in night
Yet hardly dark, and I under this day
That's scarcely light.
                        Flakes descending, dissolving
On the folds of a cape
                        on a single blue ear-ring,
On a bowler beneath the great trees of Russell Square.

III

The prim lips, homing, round the wind,
Condensing news along the Strand.
Nerveless, the words assault, descend—
Stiff jaws convey them underground.

The verb that rackets through the mind
Transports the body far beyond
Expected stops.
                Swirled on the wind
The lost, chaotic flakes ascend.

IV

All evening the princess danced, but before dawn
Escaped from her ballroom's glass down the wide, white stairs
And walked among bare trees that spiked the lawn.

Far from her ears, airy and thin, the beat
Of goldsmiths' hammers rang in Devonshire Street,
And spent, above a quarrel of barrow wheels,
Songs on the night:

> *Flakes of the outer world*
> *Through London fly*
> *Together hurled*
> *Under the heavy sky . . .*

V

I dreamt tonight that I did feast with Caesar

Wilde had been lynched. His head, grown larger, grinned from
     the Tower of London,
Swung by its hair under the Marble Arch,
And looked out from the point of a spear down Constitution Hill.
South of the River they were roasting him slowly on a spit,
And in Knightsbridge several of the best families dined delicately
     on his battered parts.
He, in Reading, enjoyed the debauch by proxy,
Bored at last with the rented corpse of Art
Whose delicate lusts had never been near to his heart.

Snow fell—fell where Hueffer ascended
From Great Russell Street to meet the eyes of Garnett;
And heard the scholar's voice: 'Now it is all ended—
England shall breed no poet for fifty years.'

Yeats not a mile from where they stood

         And Yeats
Drew down the dim blind of Olivia's hair
And dreamed of a great bird. Then woke
Calling 'Maud. Maud.' But the room was empty.

Across the narrow alley he drank coffee,
Bought his paper from me at the corner
(I only a few feet tall, in cloth cap and boots
Three sizes too large. He the toff of the buildings.)

And as he went a man approached me, shouting
'This paper you sold me—there's nothing in it'
(Waving the packed pages and snatching back his money).

And the toff, a hundred yards along the street,
And Ezra in billiard cloth trousers across the street
Wearing an ear-ring of aquamarine,
And old Possum hackneying past in a bowler to his funeral at
          the bank,

Turned
        turned, and watching, faded from sight.

VI

Now it was time for the drawing of curtains.
The smoke climbed, hand over hand, its difficult way,
Rested, or sank back in the thick air.
The River swans nor sang for the dead day
Nor proudly departed; but each hooked
One leg across its back, displaying a dirty web,
And (strong beak poised on graceful neck) poked
The rubbish drifting at the water's edge.

VII

Chanterez-vous quand vous serez vaporeuse? . . .
And as the last orange of the sun was crushed
The River accepted its lights, from Kew to Battersea
On, winding, to the Tower.

It was winter, the year '58,
And many were dead. But into the same heart and out
Through channels of stone and light, the blood still pulsed—
Carried me with it down New Oxford Street
Through Soho to the whirling clock of the Circus,
Then down, on to the bridge. The snow was freezing.
A train stood middle-poised beside the footpath
Above the water. And in a corner, hunched,
An old man's unsheathed fingers struggled to revive
The dead years on a battered violin.

A Natural Grace

Under my eaves untiring all the spring day
Two sparrows have worked with stalks the mowers leave
While I have sat regretting your going away.
All day they've ferried straw and sticks to weave
A wall against the changing moods of air,
And may have worked into that old design
A thread of cloth you wore, a strand of hair,
Since all who make are passionate for line,
Proportion, strength, and take what's near, and serves.
All day I've sat remembering your face,
And watched the sallow stalks, woven in curves
By a blind process, achieve a natural grace.

GORDON CHALLIS

The Iceman

What happened to the iceman after all?
Amazing how we waited for his call
and ran across to pick up chips of light
as the iceman's hook would beak-like bite
deep into ice, which he shouldered on a sack
and carried to our veranda at the back,
invisible the winter halo round his head.

We have other means of freezing now instead
of ice; it only lasted half a day
unwinding summer's waterclock away,
filling the tank, falling on zinc
under the icebox.

      Nowadays I think
the nameless birds outside have hauled
some massive block of silence called
the morning to my door; with beaks well ground
have started chipping splinters made of sound,
have sung me almost unaware how sick
I felt one childhood day, the embryonic
pain of seeing yolk and shell all splashed
together yellow where a bird's egg smashed;
yet pain evolves, perception grows more keen
as fits the many-coloured bird that might have been.

What happened to the iceman after all?
Amazing, how we waited for his call.

The Man of Glass

Your least and lightest movement may be critical—
not only chip your limbs and leave bright shards
but bring bang down your dazzling tower too,
cascading like piano keys sprung loose,
peeled off their cobs of octaves scales or chords.

The brittle crystal structure of your silicon,
if shattered, lacks that green organic knack
of carbon which can give and grow again;
however deft your step a stone may slip;
in bracing for the fall a bone may crack.

There is no wool nor wave will cradle your fragility;
the kindest eyes, like flux of aluminium,
look safe yet have their flashpoint, oxidize
to ash with acrid taste of alkali.
There is no way of sealing all the million

crevices that daylight makes more evident.
By night you are both captain of your soul
and lighthouse-keeper too, at home with danger,
refracting feeling into pure hues of thought,
masking those million fissures still to seal.

Yet you allow no brother-keeper's company
for you admit no brother, who by dint
of thicker skin might ward off chance collisions
(though hedgehogs dead on distant roads at night
are never really killed by accident).

And so I do not fear for you, your clumsiness,
as much as that the heat of my hand may,
no matter how well-meaning on your shoulder,
disrupt the crystals, gripping tufts of splinters,
whilst making you, in my own image, clay.

The Shadowless Man

You have to be quick to stamp out your own shadow.

So first I got to know my shadow's ductile tricks
of transformation: jet-black dwarf, diluted giant
—sometimes both at once—rotated slowly
like clock-hands as I passed
beyond the last street-lamp toward the next one,
keeping double reckoning. Every time I pounced
my shadow dodged adroitly, ducked or swerved aside.
If only I could work one jump ahead, if only
I could beat his perfect sense of timing!

Then one day I used my lethal steel-stud boots
and caught him napping, flat-footed in full sunlight,
got him good and hard right in the guts. He disappeared,
went underground a goner and good riddance.

People said: 'See here this man without a shadow,
a man through whom light shines, lies all around him,
a man more pure than rain and more transparent.'

I, however, fear another explanation:
What if I have not fully stamped him out?
(Perhaps his absence is a mere delaying)
What if the lakes are low, the power failing,
and it is my own night that keeps him waiting?

Thin Partition

Someone next door is moving things about—
dusting the shelves which don't need dusting
making changes simply for the sake of change
or hoping that new order in the room will rout
those evil demons who resent what's new and strange.

Someone next door is singing as she moves—
maybe this tune will mark the turning,
work the trick for years-old resolutions
really to come true; but then she leaves
a word amiss and spoils the spell's relations.

Someone next door is thinking what to do—
wondering what meat to buy for Sunday
or shall she go back home and try again
to hide the fact that there she feels more lonely
and knows the reason yet cannot explain.

Someone is talking to us in her way—
her shadow gestures windlike through the scrim;
my wife and I are hurried, we are going out;
someone next door is asking us to stay,
someone next door is moving things about.

The Asbestos-suited Man in Hell

A homily for saints

I can indeed afford a pause of peace,
a brief abode in shade beneath my cloak
for those, inscription-blind or heedless,
who hope that love still functions, does not choke

like sulphur in the lungs. I cannot say:
'But blow you Jack,' knowing well how far
from fireproof I am. Even this five-ply
cone of woven wet asbestos cannot bar

out heat completely. Nor in this torment
can I claim: 'I know just how you feel'
unless I am to throw away my garment
which, once parted, would not even conceal

a single sufferer beyond the grasp
of flame's bright blind yet finding fingers.
Thus, one by one, my brothers come and clasp
my calves, like children. Each soul lingers

as long as possible but finds small aid
that I should come to hell—and suffer
at my leisure, seeing meantime others wade
in pain—simply to make myself tougher.

And it is easy for me to preach salvation:
'Bring all your burning world and let me hide
you for a little while.' This insulation
shields me from all mortal sins save only pride.

The Inflammable Man

Sequel to 'The Asbestos-suited Man in Hell'

If you should seek my footprints you would find
bright crocuses of flame which mark my way
but signify no birth and burningly deter
the touch of even creatures that are blind.
The scorchmarks of these flowers formed by day
are bleached away at night as if they were

reduced by moon's cool nickel. Inert night
should on the basis of statistics be
a safer time if danger might be met
externally—a spark from steel to light
high octane, camps abandoned carelessly,
the sun through glass, a half-stubbed cigarette.

Such be the hazards which I well might fear
if I could be ignited from outside.
The masks which I must chronically don

are not to shield me, though they may appear
the same as my asbestos friend's; he tried
to keep all evil out but I have long

forsaken such a view of hell and pain;
my masks are worn to stifle what's within—
the rabid flames whose fingers never tire,
which force apart the fissures till again
a new mask must be laid, where one burns thin,
to feed and hide the anarchy of fire.

The Postman

This cargo of confessions, messages,
demands to pay, seems none of my concern;
you could say I'm a sort of go-between
for abstract agents trusting wheels will turn,
for censored voices stilled in space and time.

Some people stop me for a special letter;
one or two will tell me, if it's fine, that I
have picked the right job for this kind of weather.
A boy who understands life somewhat better
asks where postmen live—if not our office, why?

The work is quite routine but kindnesses
and awkward problems crop up now and then:
one old lady sometimes startles passers-by
claiming she is blameless as she hisses
at people present in her reminiscent ken;

she startled me as well the other day,
gave me a glass of lemonade and slipped
me a letter to deliver—'Don't you say
a word to anyone, it's no concern
of theirs, or yours.' Nor no more it was, except

here was this letter plainly marked 'To God'
and therefore insufficiently addressed.
I cannot stamp it now 'Return to sender'
for addressee and sender may be One. The best
thing is burn it, to a black rose He'll remember.

The Thermostatic Man

The world could fall to pieces any moment now;
with luck it won't,
mainly because it hasn't yet. Though cracks appear,
I'll merely count
them leeway spaces left so masses may expand
to meet and don't.

But I, who used to walk bolt upright, this day bow
as meek as wheat:
how can I be sure I shall not always fear
to face fierce heat,
to face the sun, not watch my shadow lagging back behind,
and feel complete?

From strips of many metals am I made. I grow
beneath the sun
unevenly. I cannot cry lest the least tear
should cool down one
soft element and strain the others. I am bland,
bend to become

the thermostat which keeps my spirit burning low.
One day I shall
perhaps be tried by a more humble, human fire
which, blending all
my elements in one alloy, will let me stand
upright, ready to fall.

298

The Oracle

One-time liaison officer in Babel's tower,
I prophesy in any tongue; and in your voice
I hear both answers—one your question craves,
the other unacceptable. The prophets truer
to their trade would not shirk words that grieve,
nor care to be believed. However, their advice

is hard to come by and, when sought, neglected
like disused diamond mines where they retire.
They offer truth, more hard than any stone,
which trimmed to shape traps light within refracted
but when reduced to crystal thin-ness shows its own
extinction angle, just like any stone; its fire

is swampwards lost back in the lairs of time.
Meanwhile a lesser substance came from those swamp trees:
here I inhabit galleries where coal was mined
and, though the pit's redundant, people climb
down these shafts, like shifts of miners, bent to find
some little fuel for their dreams before they freeze.

Yet my advice is neither coloured black as coal
nor white as ash; the truth half-told suffices,
being the only kind that calls for full belief.
And if I say that you must seek your soul
where waves begin, beyond the hidden reef,
you still may choose to put away the crisis

of choosing till another day, the weather
being unpropitious and the route through pain.
Or, like most, you may interpret me to mean
'go such a way, seek this sign or that other,'
and then you'll thank me, ask what sacrifice has been
ordained. There was a sacrifice . . . You came.

KEVIN IRELAND

Parade: Liberation Day

Think of a tree-lined city street
on an early autumn day;
fashion placards and bunting;
imagine a display
of dripping clothes
drying among the flags and signs
hung from the balconies;
think flags on to washing-lines.

People this street;
create language and breed.
Then think of, say, twenty tanks,
cornering at a terrifying speed,
powdering the paving-bricks;
imagine parachutes, drifting like thistle seed
through the gusts of autumn leaves and sticks.

Now picture the infantry,
young, strong,
measuring with hobnails
their heroic song.
Yet make this song trail from the distance,
though the soldiers are near:
the rhythm is significant,
the words need not be clear.

Think of a happy street
on an early autumn night;
imagine tables and chairs beneath the trees,
and the gay light
of coloured globes,
swaying with flag and sign.

People this street;
create chatter and wine.
Then think of, say, a billion stars,
and a moon darting at a terrifying speed
from darkness, to darkness again.
Erase it all
with sudden drenching rain.

Now picture the infantry,
cold, damp,
measuring with hobnails
the way back to camp.
Yet make their tread trail from the distance,
though they are near:
gently imagine them,
their future is not clear.

Deposition

I cannot
give you words
which turned
as succulent as flesh
upon the nib:

thin men
write gaunt poems
and each word
sticks out
like a rib

Striking a Pose

we'll stock up books
and wine and pie
then stop the clocks
and never die

we'll nail the windows
brick up the door
and live on a mattress
on the floor

if death still comes
we'll strike a pose
and hold our breath
until he goes

A Hidden Message

her kiss on the mirror
was crushed and mute:
why couldn't she simply
leave a note?

I rubbed at her lipstick
and met my eye:
and got the message
hidden away

Educating the Body

when she asked
her sudden: why?
she tricked no answer
from my eye

when she tried
to make me slip
she forced no stammer
from my lip

she tried to joke
to sting to trip
her efforts could not
shake my grip

what should she do
with one so sly?
even my body
learns to lie

A Popular Romance

will you have me?
groaned the frog
my squashy love
is all agog

do you care?
complained the crab
a true heart serves
this horny scab

the prince exclaimed
if you agree
your love could change
the brute in me

they're all the same
the princess said
it's like a bestiary
in my bed

PETER BLAND

Death of a Dog

Sally is dead, and the children stand around
Like small white lilies. Someone,
In a terrible hurry, has ground
Her red tongue into unaccustomed silence.
Now, all that was so much living
Lies like a mound of wet rags—freezing
Beneath my daughter's rough excited hands.

It is no risk for her, this going near
A silence she cannot understand.
Frank as forever she has wandered out
Beyond all thought of our complaining
And stands there pouting—puzzled to believe
That one who partners her adventures
Still lies at daybreak in a tangled sleep.

I tell her this is death, and leave
It at that. She does not weep
But runs repeating what she's learned
To all who'll listen. Women up the street
Spare kindness—grief quickens them
Like a cup of tea. Their men,
More urgently, cram early buses . . .

Life bursts into diesel oil and nicotine.
She feels her message meets with mild reproof
And so returns to that child-crowded scene
Where all was black and white, but finds
Someone's removed the death she runs to greet.
Tonight there'll be a burying, and tomorrow
A gap in the world to watch her cram with pleasure.

Mother

(Died September 1950, Stone, Staffordshire)

Last night came calling out of the dark
Your reborn image . . .
                              Mother, Mother,
Stretched between two wars and drained
By a crop of cancer . . . I thought I heard
Your brass voice laughing with my drowned
Sea brother. In my dream you nursed
His salt-lungs back to manhood; when
The guns exploded you blew back the waves
From his wrecked mouth. Again, I named
Your loud love to the factory hurt
And council-house heart of England—breathing
The warmth of your hennaed hair
Above the smell of earth. Beside your grave
I danced to your favourite tango and lowered
Your sky-blue pyjamas from the steeple,
While all about me sailors and factory girls
Coupled beneath the trees, and crocuses
Sprang from your buried death's black flower.

Past the Tin Butterflies and Plaster Gnomes

Past the tin butterflies and plaster gnomes,
The home-maid garages, the weekend roasts,
The cats' paws delicate in new-laid concrete,
The cast-off sheaths and ice-cream cones
Outside the phone-box, and a mist of screams
Clouding the blue above the net-ball courts,
Past pastel avenues and rainbow houses,
Past father fuelling at the Bottle Store,
Past the Chemist Shop and the Corner Dairy
And the family photos on the kitchen walls,

305

Past clocks and mirrors and the coloured pictures
Of *Nature's Wonderland*—all sheep and snow,
And home in time to switch the radio over
From *This is New Zealand* to *My Orphaned Soul*.

Remembering England

Often the sudden smell of 'home'
sexed up in some angry northern novel
sours my blood. I remember most
wet council-house walls of pale distemper.
Was there anger there . . . in that fungus growth;
myself as a post-war adolescent?
I taste the damp, recurring thought
of being bred to expect so little.

No wonder, then, that our lives congeal
when we settle here like convalescents
to blink in this hard light and build
our hospital-homes of sun and butter.
What more *could* we want . . . the journey done
and hygiene triumphant over passion?
And that remains is to play the nurse
in this sanatorium for British anger.

Kumara God

Three days and still the slow fogged rain
Drifts inland—all along the valley
Light melts to clusters of steamed-up panes.
All's formlessness—a sharpened will
Won't chip us free of it. It is
A melting back, an elemental drift
Beyond time or season . . .

                And so I bring
The little stone cramped kumara god
In from the garden . . . Take down the clock
And set him there, upon the mantelpiece,
To be my curled-in self, grown
Old in embryo, slightly sardonic . . .
Feeling around me this slow retreat
Of lives gone underground, of sleep turned solid.

So Many Cenotaphs

So many cenotaphs! As though a people
Had come here just to be remembered;
Finding no other future but to fall
Somewhere else and for some other quarrel
Than that which brought them. So,
To atone for leaving . . . to leave again;
And for that Fall . . . to Fall.

              So much dead stone!
As though a people, turning back to wave,
Stepped out into their own memorials.

The Happy Army

The child has a vision of the happy army. He
has carefully sketched in my appointment book
the smiles, the fingers, the boots and guns
his happy army wave like rattles. No
one is dying, no one's bad or good
and even the one at the back has a medal
while the generals beam pure love. The sun
has rolled to the ground, has been caught up
in a growing air of excitement that runs
riot, filling the earth with faces, arms, legs
and bits of old tanks. It is natural
that everyone, everywhere, faces the front,
not out of discipline or to scare the enemy
but in frank expectancy of applause. And
of course this is why this particular army
is happy, why no one dies, why the sun
shares in the happy army's happiness
and rolls down to earth. It is why I run
towards the boots and guns, why I come
as far as I dare to the edge of the paper
to stare . . . to stare and to cheer them on.

FLEUR ADCOCK

Wife to Husband

From anger into the pit of sleep
You go with a sudden skid. On me
Stillness falls gradually, a soft
Snowfall, a light cover to keep
Numb for a time the twitching nerves.

Your head on the pillow is turned away;
My face is hidden. But under snow
Shoots uncurl, the green thread curves
Instinctively upwards. Do not doubt
That sense of purpose in mindless flesh:
Between our bodies a warmth grows;
Under the blankets hands move out,
Your back touches my breast, our thighs
Turn to find their accustomed place.

Your mouth is moving over my face:
Do we dare, now, to open our eyes?

For a Five-Year-Old

A snail is climbing up the window-sill
Into your room, after a night of rain.
You call me in to see, and I explain
That it would be unkind to leave it there:
It might crawl to the floor; we must take care
That no one squashes it. You understand,
And carry it outside, with careful hand,
To eat a daffodil.

I see, then, that a kind of faith prevails:
Your gentleness is moulded still by words
From me, who have trapped mice and shot wild birds,
From me, who drowned your kittens, who betrayed
Your closest relatives, and who purveyed
The harshest kind of truth to many another.
But that is how things are: I am your mother,
And we are kind to snails.

Note on Propertius I.5

Among the Roman love-poets, possession
Is a rare theme. The locked and flower-hung door,
The shivering lover, are allowed. To more
Buoyant moods, the canons of expression
Gave grudging sanction. Do we, then, assume,
Finding Propertius tear-sodden and jealous,
That Cynthia was inexorably callous?
Plenty of moonlight entered that high room
Whose doors had met his Alexandrine battles;
And she, so gay a lutanist, was known
To stitch and doze a night away, alone,
Until the poet tumbled in with apples
For penitence and for her head his wreath,
Brought from a party, of wine-scented roses—
(The garland's aptness lying, one supposes,
Less in the flowers than in the thorns beneath:
Her waking could, he knew, provide his verses
With less idyllic themes.) On to her bed
He rolled the round fruit, and adorned her head;
Then gently roused her sleeping mouth to curses.
Here the conventions reassert their power:
The apples fall and bruise, the roses wither,
Touched by a sallowed moon. But there were other
Luminous nights—(even the cactus flower

Glows briefly golden, fed by spiny flesh)—
And once, as he acknowledged, all was singing:
The moonlight musical, the darkness clinging,
And she compliant to his every wish.

from *Night-Piece*

2. Before Sleep

Lying close to your heart-beat, my lips
Touching the pulse in your neck, my head on your arm,
I listen to your hidden blood as it slips
With a small furry sound along the warm
Veins; and my slowly-flowering dream
Of Chinese landscapes, river-banks and flying
Splits into sudden shapes—children who scream
By a roadside, blinded men, a woman lying
In a bed filled with blood: the broken ones.
We are so vulnerable. I curl towards
That intricate machine of nerves and bones
With its built-in life: your body. And to your words
I whisper 'Yes' and 'Always', as I lie
Waiting for thunder from a stony sky.

Incident

When you were lying on the white sand,
A rock under your head, and smiling,
(Circled by dead shells), I came to you
And you said, reaching to take my hand,
'Lie down.' So for a time we lay
Warm on the sand, talking and smoking,
Easy; while the grovelling sea behind
Sucked at the rocks and measured the day.
Lightly I fell asleep then, and fell
Into a cavernous dream of falling.

It was all the cave-myths, it was all
The myths of tunnel or tower or well—
Alice's rabbit-hole into the ground,
Or the path of Orpheus: a spiral staircase
To hell, furnished with danger and doubt.
Stumbling, I suddenly woke; and found
Water about me. My hair was wet,
And you were sitting on the grey sand,
Waiting for the lapping tide to take me:
Watching, and lighting a cigarette.

Unexpected Visit

I have nothing to say about this garden.
I do not want to be here, I can't explain
What happened. I merely opened a usual door
And found this. The rain

Has just stopped, and the gravel paths are trickling
With water. Stone lions, on each side,
Gleam like wet seals, and the green birds
Are stiff with dripping pride.

Not my kind of country. The gracious vistas,
The rose-gardens and terraces, are all wrong—
As comfortless as the weather. But here I am.
I cannot tell how long

I have stood gazing at grass too wet to sit on,
Under a sky so dull I cannot read
The sundial, staring along the curving walks
And wondering where they lead;

Not really hoping, though, to be enlightened.
It must be morning, I think, but there is no
Horizon behind the trees, no sun as clock
Or compass. I shall go

And find, somewhere among the formal hedges
Or hidden behind a trellis, a toolshed. There
I can sit on a box and wait. Whatever happens
May happen anywhere,

And better, perhaps, among the rakes and flowerpots
And sacks of bulbs than under this pallid sky:
Having chosen nothing else, I can at least
Choose to be warm and dry.

For Andrew

'Will I die?' you ask. And so I enter on
The dutiful exposition of that which you
Would rather not know, and I rather not tell you.
To soften my 'Yes' I offer compensations—
Age and fulfilment ('It's so far away;
You will have children and grandchildren by then')
And indifference ('By then you will not care').
No need: you cannot believe me, convinced
That if you always eat plenty of vegetables,
And are careful crossing the street, you will live for ever.
And so we close the subject, with much unsaid—
This, for instance: Though you and I may die
Tomorrow or next year, and nothing remain
Of our stock, of the unique, preciously-hoarded
Inimitable genes we carry in us,
It is possible that for many generations
There will exist, sprung from whatever seeds,
Children straight-limbed, with clear inquiring voices,
Bright-eyed as you. Or so I like to think:
Sharing in this your childish optimism.

Composition for Words and Paint

This darkness has a quality
That poses us in shapes and textures,
One plane behind another,
Flatness in depth.

Your face; a fur of hair; a striped
Curtain behind, and to one side cushions;
Nothing recedes, all lies extended.
I sink upon your image.

I see a soft metallic glint,
A tinsel weave behind the canvas,
Aluminium and bronze beneath the ochre.
There is more in this than we know.

I can imagine drawn around you
A white line, in delicate brush-strokes:
Emphasis; but you do not need it.
You have completeness.

I am not measuring your gestures;
(I have seen you measure those of others,
Know a mind by a hand's trajectory,
The curve of a lip.)

But you move, and I move towards you,
Draw back your head, and I advance.
I am fixed to the focus of your eyes.
I share your orbit.

Now I discover things about you:
Your thin wrists, a tooth missing;
And how I melt and burn before you.
I have known you always.

The greyness from the long windows
Reduces visual depth; but tactile
Reality defines half-darkness.
My hands prove you solid.

You draw me down upon your body,
Hard arms behind my head.
Darkness and soft colours blur.
We have swallowed the light.

Now I dissolve you in my mouth,
Catch in the corners of my throat
The sly taste of your love, sliding
Into me, singing.

Just as the birds have started singing.
Let them come flying through the windows
With chains of opals around their necks.
We are expecting them.

The Water Below

This house is floored with water,
Wall to wall, a deep green pit,
Still and gleaming, edged with stone.
Over it are built stairways
And railed living-areas
In wrought iron. All rather
Impractical; it will be
Damp in winter, and we shall
Surely drop small objects—keys,
Teaspoons, or coins—through the chinks
In the ironwork, to splash
Lost into the glimmering
Depths (and do we know how deep?)

It will have to be rebuilt:
A solid floor of concrete
Over this dark well (perhaps
Already full of coins, like
The flooded crypt of that church
In Ravenna). You might say
It could be drained, made into
A useful cellar for coal.
But I am sure the water
Would return; would never go.
Under my grandmother's house
In Drury, when I was three,
I always believed there was
Water: lift up the floorboards
And you would see it—a lake,
A subterranean sea.
True, I played under the house
And saw only hard-packed earth,
Wooden piles, gardening tools,
A place to hunt for lizards.
That was different: below
I saw no water. Above,
I knew it must still be there,
Waiting. (For why did we say
'Forgive us our trespasses,
Deliver us from evil?')
Always beneath the safe house
Lies the pool, the hidden sea
Created before we were.
It is not easy to drain
The waters under the earth.

VINCENT O'SULLIVAN

Elegy for a Schoolmate

On the other side of the world I heard
That she died in a Newton kitchen,
Her head in someone else's oven.

I'd never thumped her nor called her names
With the others, and so I had nothing
To sorrow or anger about.

                  Her big
Wet-nosed face just the same for me
As if she was sitting in the desk beside me.

Her clothes were always dirty
And she said stupid things.
The stupidest when she was trying hardest.

And I wish now that I'd thrown
A rock at her, had her caned for smoking . . .
Then I could feel pent-up for a day
          And forget her.

But she takes her place among immortal things.
With the potter's wheel at the bottom of a dry pit,
With the hands of Egyptian ladies held like thin,
   brown leaves,
Their collars of beaten gold, and a basalt dog.

Which Wing the Angel Chooses

Which wing the angel chooses
To flick us with, michaelean
Or post-satanic, is no casual quibble,
No field for aged divines to pasture on.
It is a thought our minds are hot with.

Provocation at the purest corners,
White vision in riot's crowded market,
You walk like the demon in medieval dream,
Saint to the eye, until night unbuttons
Your true intent.

Then oh your body burns like a candle flame,
Raises desire like an eager Lazarus,
While your crossings, all left-handed,
Your vestments black, draw blood
Like a thread of silk through coldest veins.

Conundrum, succubus, terror to small hours,
Daylight's appraisal places you again
In gothic niche, sets you on mind's reredos
Ready to summon prayer, promise
In your steady eye of gentler ways.

Like this, you could stand naked
In a crowd, and swing its lust to virtue,
Make temples of your either breast,
Incite to pilgrimage, entice response.
This terrifies as surely.

But to catch you in the quirky light,
One side turned rosy with demonic flares,
The other a jacket of civil graces,
Is our supplication; to find sanctuary
In your bosom, deceit in your joined hands.

Medusa

Sits at the window, waits the threatened steel
as any common housewife waits near dark
for groceries that should have come at four,
when it's too late to phone to hear they're certain,
to know the boy is pedalling up the hill
and not gone home. A boy who's late—
it could be simply that, so still her hands.

Two or three birds. Bare branches.
A thrush taps on the gravel, tilts its head.
Her eyes, she thinks, could hold it if she wanted,
could make it come up close, think this is home.
Sits there, her hands folded, her lips cold,
the expected blade already on her skin.

A piece of wind no bigger than a man
moves the dead leaves, bends the sopping grass.
A blind cord knocks the window like a drum.
'Perseus, stalwart, honest, comes his way,
his footstep nicks the corners of the day,
like something hard against a grey, chipped stone.'
The stone he says she makes with those grey eyes.
Jade in the dusk. Heavier than grey.

And when he comes, how talk moves like a mirror,
a polished shield, in shadows, then in light,
always his care to stay behind its hurt.
Talks of her greatest gift—to deck out men
in stone: stone heart, stone limbs, the lot.
Turns men to stone, turns them to herself.
'The only way to end, for both our good.'
And like a man who shows off coins or gems
he lets his words fall in the room by ones,
and twos, or if in piles, it's when
their rushing sounds and feels a streaming sword.
Edges in close with that, to do his work.
And all her strength, to keep her eyes from his.

Clown, and all the sea behind him

He's very odd, standing on yellow sand.
His grey and crimson, satin, three-inch diamonds

agitate the smallest children most.
The older ones keep saying it's plain silly,

but they know, these others, it's more elaborate madness.
It's planned before like the concrete tower's planned

to hide the sun in the mornings. See him turning now
like the steps that go round the tower and round the sky.

The diamonds over his heart are stained, like tea
that's spilt on a patchwork quilt, and made it run.

He shouldn't have ever come to the beach like that.
He's got sand as well in his pom-poms,

that ugly stain, and his hat's lost somewhere, surely.
Only spiky hair, a kind of dirty grass.

When you ask him to take a pigeon from under his arm
he lifts his arm and laughs when nothing happens.

'So, he's been drinking has he?' a father says.
The girls are called to come back and his coloured diamonds

go shiny click this way, dark, dark, that,
until he moves so quickly, going round,

he's winding the afternoon sun like a wire on him,
he's a reel with yards and yards of sunset to him.

His costume's gone to his mind. Leave him alone.
A clown, and all the sea behind him.

He's a bird turning his cage to another bird.

The Children

We are the children born
with tongues leafy as old lettuces.

Our green eyes are a fire
that had burned right down before we saw it,

our hands blue
like the Virgin's holy mantle

because we have held them up,
oh, ever so long,
against the sky.

Or brown, from pressing all night
against varnished doors.

When we walk along the road,
nothing ever happens.

The puddles stay as wet as ever,
dust falls from the pines onto our heads.
And the youngest of us say 'perfume, perfume!'
and will skip as the word pleases,
say '*bijoux*' and '*oiseaux*'
and in open daylight
jump at the sounds as though we were in a tunnel.

We are the children
who know the tricks of silence,
the cold minutes stacked to make an igloo.

Why do we think the sun
is a dirty coin?
why do we envy the yellow garters
on the skinny wasps?

Come inside, come inside,
it's late and we hadn't noticed.
Don't you know
the big white plates are watching for us?

K. O. ARVIDSON

The Tall Wind

He said to them, Look at this: you see
Where the tall wind leans against your window-pane?
And they said Yes; the cold has come again.
Which being true, he could not disagree.

Instead he said, If that wind once more blows
Like that, your house will fly away like straw;
But they, of course, had thought of that before.
And also, though he did not dare suppose

They might have done, they'd seen a dead man lain
For laundering on half a fallen tree.
He thought, How strangely that man looks like me;
And said aloud, With luck we'll miss the rain . . .

And just as he spoke it started in to pour.
One of them laughed, and one said, Thar she blows;
We'll find out now what this young charlie knows:
There's a tall wind out there, leaning on our door.

Fish and Chips on the Merry-Go-Round

In caves with a single purpose
Fish were drawn deliberately
From room to room.
Pallid Romans employed them
In a kind of masonry.
They even had their own day of the week.
Before that, though,
Presumably,
Before the nails from Calvary went back
Like bullets into the dove on Ararat,

323

There must have been a fish or two
Sharked many a household bare:
Great bloated sunfish, ogling octopi,
Between the bedstead and the hearth with relish
Tearing apart all shining arkless men,
Competing for the viscous eyeballs loose
Like opals on the suffocated floor.

A seasonable peripety assures
Contemporary hygiene,
Symbol and ancestor alike
Hosed out, or splintered off.

Little, or large as eels, fish
Fodder us; best of all
On the six days in between.
They build us up.

Still,
On a slow wheel, sharpening fins
Give glints.

from *The Flame Tree*

You might at one time, when you were young perhaps,
Have imagined that by holding out your hand
You could seize the moon.
Reconstructing the attempt, you might recall
How, silent at first, and single, the moon,
Avoiding your hand that moved like a cloud across it,
Prickled at length on the dryness of your eyes,
And split to a raffish galaxy, rapid and menacing,
Invading you at last through the holes of your head;
Acrid, intemperate brilliance
Racketing
With a scream of engines.

And in dense quiet then, the solitary moon
Watched
As the veins were flooded in your hand.

What gazing now can turn us into gods,
Lightning at our command?

from *The Last Songs of Richard Strauss*
  at Takahe above the Kaipara

  3. Im Abendrot (*von Eichendorff*)

The far Brynderwyns heave across the harbour,
rising upon the second tide, mountains
in mangrove moving, weaving
the last complexities of the sun. These
are a tangle of reflections. Over them,
the next peninsula shines yellow,
pastoral century of slow change,
and the roofs of pioneers, like beacons, prophesy
the imminence of fishermen, their lights
alive and casting, quick
to be out before the strong tide sucks and runs.

I sing of our long voyaging,
and you who led me, at my side;
I sing the saddest of all things;
I sing the unaccomplished bride.

The hills will cease to float soon, and the mangroves
ripple themselves away.
The wandering flames of grass will calm, and the cattle
boom night's gullies up and down. My lights
will anchor a headland. Boats will take bearings,
seeking the channel; and then,
the Kaipara will move out.

A shag clap-claps in shallows.
I point the way to an open sea,
though all my doors are closed,
and I within.

Go slowly, sun. A gentle death
of day is in the birds that wheel
in clouds to their accustomed rest,
and in the racing of the keel

before the racing of the tide,
and in the crowding of dark trees.
I sing the unaccomplished bride.
I sing my death in all of these.

MICHAEL JACKSON

Art Market: Leopoldville

Taking this painting at an appropriate distance
I see my critical eye was a loaded dice
in an empty cup looking for a winner
and his face comes back to me
the black fellow who spoke of poverty
and sat down as I sipped an iced martini
near the market, first day of the rains.

The four-month drought had broken
they said, as usual, according to a full moon
and when the downpour and the grey skies came
I knew the clouds in the blue one day before
must have inspired in me an old nostalgia
remembering closed windows, curtains drawn
in a warm room, and friends arriving to talk
and stay and hear Beethoven in the afternoon.

The painting is of a flood, a sunset
reminiscent of Turner, and some crudely delineated
fishing traps, giving on to a canoe
and its lonely occupant pushing an oar,
and it's a bad painting, lacks composition
and the colouring is poor,
water and sky contradicting, in fact
the whole thing the work of an amateur
and not worth nine hundred francs.

Yet that is what I gave and would have given
   more,
the first price named, broke as I was
when he bargained for bread,
and my head reeling with booze

told me against it as I said
I'll take it, you've a lot to learn
but you're young, hungry and untaught
and I've only money in Africa to burn.

Fille de Joie: Congo

Lips caked with lipstick
And the smell of booze
You dance with the man of ten thousand francs
Until the music moves him to
Take you to the room where the rite will be.

Preferring him not
To put out the light
You remove a bonnet of dead women's hair
Beneath which you jealously preserve
Stiff twirls of the African *coiffure*.

Down to your silken underthings
Breasts astir
And his own undoing scarcely seen
You are the cur under midnight heat
Of a mad dog doing it
For what in Europe would have been love.

Return from Luluabourg

My report is not of schools
We built out there, or market gardens
Planted to help the poor
But of an evening after work
When through a ruined iron gate I saw
A garden overgrown with weeds
And entered it.

Before me rusting boats, swings
Dislodged like giants on a dungeon rack,
Seesaws split, unpainted, thrown aside,
A wall from which I could not turn my back,
My own hands tied.

That concrete prison drop was set
With broken glass along the top,
Bottles once put to European lips
At evening on a *patio*.
I climbed a metal staircase,
Looked across a land scarred red,
Huts roofed with grass on which
White bone-like mango roots were dried
To rid them of their arsenic.

But poisons which had touched that place
Still kept it out of bounds;
Pleasures had gone, children's voices
Were not heard
Except beyond that wall, in villages
Or in the dusk, the garden, one night bird.

BIBLIOGRAPHY

New Zealand may be assumed to be the place of publication
unless otherwise stated

ARTHUR H. ADAMS
Maoriland: and other Verses, The Bulletin Newspaper Company,
   Sydney, 1899.
The Nazarene: A Study of a Man, Philip Wellby, 1902.
London Streets, T. N. Foulis, London, 1906.
The Collected Verses of Arthur H. Adams, Whitcombe and Tombs, 1913.
My Friend Remember, Angus and Robertson, Sydney, 1915.

FLEUR ADCOCK
The Eye of the Hurricane, A. H. and A. W. Reed, 1964.
Tigers, Oxford University Press, London, 1967.

B. E. BAUGHAN
Verses, Constable, London, 1898.
Reuben and Other Poems, Constable, London, 1903.
Shingle-short and Other Verses, Whitcombe and Tombs, 1908.
Hope: A Poem, privately published, 1916?
Poems from the Port Hills, Whitcombe and Tombs, 1923.

JAMES K. BAXTER
Beyond the Palisade, Caxton Press, 1944.
Blow, Wind of Fruitfulness, Caxton Press, 1948.
Poems Unpleasant (with Anton Vogt and Louis Johnson), Pegasus
   Press, 1952.
The Iron Breadboard, Studies in New Zealand Writing, Mermaid Press,
   1957.
The Night Shift, Poems on Aspects of Love (with Charles Doyle, Louis
   Johnson, and Kendrick Smithyman), Capricorn Press, 1957.
In Fires of No Return, Oxford University Press, London, 1958.
Howrah Bridge and Other Poems, Oxford University Press, London,
   1961.
Pig-Island Letters, Oxford University Press, London, 1966.
The Lion Skin, Otago University Press, 1967.
The Rock Woman: Selected Poems, Oxford University Press, London,
   1969.

MARY URSULA BETHELL
From a Garden in the Antipodes, by Evelyn Hayes [pseud.], Sidgwick
   and Jackson, London, 1929.
Time and Place, Caxton Press, 1936.
Day and Night, Poems 1924-34, Caxton Press, 1939.
Collected Poems, Caxton Press, 1950.

PETER BLAND

Habitual Fevers in *3 Poets* (with John Boyd and Victor O'Leary), Capricorn Press, 1958.
Domestic Interiors, Wai-Te-Ata Press, 1964.
My Side of the Story, Poems 1960–1964, Mate Books, 1964.

CHARLES BRASCH

The Land and the People and Other Poems, Caxton Press, 1939.
The Quest, a verse play, The Compass Players, London, 1946.
Disputed Ground, Poems 1939–45, Caxton Press, 1948.
The Estate and Other Poems, Caxton Press, 1957.
Ambulando, Caxton Press, 1964.
Not Far Off, Caxton Press, 1969.

ALISTAIR CAMPBELL

Mine Eyes Dazzle, Poems 1947–9, Pegasus Press, 1950; revised editions, 1951 and 1956.
Sanctuary of Spirits, Wai-Te-Ata Press, 1963.
Wild Honey, Oxford University Press, London, 1964.
Blue Rain, Wai-Te-Ata Press, 1967.

GORDON CHALLIS

Building, Caxton Press, 1963.

ALLEN CURNOW

Valley of Decision, Phoenix Miscellany I, Auckland University College Students' Association, 1933.
Three Poems, Caxton Press, 1935.
Enemies, Poems 1934–36, Caxton Club Press, 1937.
Not in Narrow Seas, Caxton Press, 1939.
Recent Poems (with A. R. D. Fairburn, Denis Glover, and R. A. K. Mason), Caxton Press, 1941.
Island and Time, Caxton Press, 1941.
Sailing or Drowning, Progressive Publishing Society, 1943.
Jack Without Magic, Caxton Press, 1946.
At Dead Low Water, and Sonnets, Caxton Press, 1949.
The Axe: A Verse Tragedy, Caxton Press, 1949.
edited, *A Book of New Zealand Verse, 1923–45*, Caxton Press, 1945; revised edition, 1951.
Poems 1949–57, Mermaid Press, 1957.
The Penguin Book of New Zealand Verse, edited for Penguin Books, London, 1960.
A Small Room with Large Windows, Oxford University Press, London, 1962.

RUTH DALLAS

Country Road and Other Poems, 1947–52, Caxton Press, 1953.
The Turning Wheel, Caxton Press, 1961.
Day Book, Caxton Press, 1966.
Shadow Show, Caxton Press, 1968.

BASIL DOWLING
A Day's Journey, Caxton Press, 1941.
Signs and Wonders, Caxton Press, 1944.
Canterbury and Other Poems, Caxton Press, 1949.
Hatherley, Recollective Lyrics, University of Otago Press, 1968.

CHARLES DOYLE
A Splinter of Glass, Pegasus Press, 1956.
The Night Shift, Poems on Aspects of Love (with James K. Baxter, Louis Johnson, and Kendrick Smithyman), Capricorn Press, 1957.
Distances, Paul's Book Arcade, 1963.
Recent Poetry in New Zealand, edited for Collins, 1965.
Messages for Herod, Collins, 1965.
A Sense of Place; poems, Wai-Te-Ata Press, 1965.
Earth Meditations: 2, Charles Alldritt, 1968.

EILEEN DUGGAN
Poems, The New Zealand Tablet, 1922.
New Zealand Bird Songs, H. H. Tombs, 1929.
Poems, Allen and Unwin, London, 1937.
New Zealand Poems, Allen and Unwin, London, 1940.
More Poems, Allen and Unwin, London, 1951.

A. R. D. FAIRBURN
He Shall Not Rise, Columbia Press, London, 1930.
Dominion, Caxton Press, 1938.
Recent Poems (with Allen Curnow, Denis Glover, and R. A. K. Mason), Caxton Press, 1941.
Poems 1929–1941, Caxton Press, 1943.
The Rakehelly Man, Caxton Press, 1946.
Three Poems: Dominion, The Voyage, To a Friend in the Wilderness, New Zealand University Press, 1952.
Strange Rendezvous, Poems 1929–1941, with additions, Caxton Press, 1952.
The Disadvantages of Being Dead, Mermaid Press, 1958.
Poetry Harbinger (with Denis Glover), Pilgrim Press, 1958.
Collected Poems, Pegasus Press, 1966.

JANET FRAME
The Pocket Mirror, Pegasus Press, 1967.

DENIS GLOVER
Thistledown, Caxton Club Press, 1935.
Six Easy Ways of Dodging Debt Collectors, Caxton Press, 1936.
The Arraignment of Paris, Caxton Press, 1937.
Thirteen Poems, Caxton Press, 1939.
Cold Tongue, Caxton Press, 1940.
Recent Poems (with Allen Curnow, A. R. D. Fairburn, and R. A. K. Mason), Caxton Press, 1941.
The Wind and the Sand, Poems 1934–44, Caxton Press, 1945.
Summer Flowers, Caxton Press, 1946.
Sings Harry and Other Poems, Caxton Press, 1951.

Arawata Bill: A Sequence of Poems, Pegasus Press, 1953.
Since Then, Mermaid Press, 1957.
Poetry Harbinger (with A. R. D. Fairburn), Pilgrim Press, 1958.
Enter Without Knocking, Pegasus Press, 1964.
Sharp Edge Up, Verses and Satires, Paul, 1968.

PAUL HENDERSON (RUTH FRANCE)
Unwilling Pilgrim, Caxton Press, 1955.
The Halting Place, Caxton Press, 1961.

J. R. HERVEY
Selected Poems, Caxton Press, 1940.
New Poems, Caxton Press, 1942.
Man on a Raft, More Poems, Caxton Press, 1949.
She Was My Spring, Caxton Press, 1955.

ROBIN HYDE (IRIS GUIVER WILKINSON)
The Desolate Star, Whitcombe and Tombs, 1929.
The Conquerors, Macmillan, London, 1935.
Persephone in Winter, Hurst and Blackell, 1937.
Houses by the Sea and the Later Poems of Robin Hyde, Caxton Press, 1952.

KEVIN IRELAND
Face to Face, Pegasus Press, 1963.
Educating the Body, Caxton Press, 1967.

LOUIS JOHNSON
Stanza and Scene, Handcraft Press, 1945.
The Sun Among the Ruins, Pegasus Press, 1951.
Roughshod Among the Lilies, Pegasus Press, 1951.
Poems Unpleasant (with James K. Baxter and Anton Vogt), 1952.
The Dark Glass, Handcraft Press, 1955.
Two Poems, Pegasus Press, 1956.
New Worlds for Old, Capricorn Press, 1957.
The Night Shift, Poems on Aspects of Love (with James K. Baxter, Charles Doyle, and Kendrick Smithyman), Capricorn Press, 1957.
New Zealand Poetry Yearbook, editor, vols. I–III, Reed, 1951–3; vols. IV–XI, Pegasus Press, 1954–62, 1964.
Bread and A Pension, Pegasus Press, 1964.

M. K. JOSEPH
Imaginary Islands, the author, 1950.
The Living Countries, Paul's Book Arcade, 1959.

KATHERINE MANSFIELD
Poems, Constable, London, 1923.
To Stanislaw Wyspianski, privately printed for Bertram Rota, Bodley House, 1938.

R. A. K. MASON
In the Manner of Men, the author, 1923.
The Beggar, the author, 1924.
Penny Broadsheet, the author, 1925.
No New Thing—Poems 1924–29, Spearhead, 1934.

End of Day, Caxton Press, 1936.
Squire Speaks, Caxton Press, 1938.
This Dark Will Lighten, Selected Poems 1923–41, Caxton Press, 1941.
China, privately published, 1943.
Collected Poems, Pegasus Press, 1962.

W. H. OLIVER
Fire Without Phoenix, Poems 1946–54, Caxton Press, 1957.

VINCENT O'SULLIVAN
Our Burning Time, Prometheus Books, 1965.
Revenants, Prometheus Books, 1969.

GLORIA RAWLINSON
Gloria's Book, Whitcombe and Tombs, 1933.
The Perfume Vendor, Hutchinson, London, 1936.
The Islands Where I Was Born, Handcraft Press, 1955.
Of Clouds and Pebbles, Paul's Book Arcade, 1963.

KEITH SINCLAIR
Songs for a Summer, Pegasus Press, 1952.
Strangers or Beasts, Caxton Press, 1954.
A Time to Embrace, Paul's Book Arcade, 1963.

KENDRICK SMITHYMAN
Seven Sonnets, Pelorus Press, 1946.
The Blind Mountain, Caxton Press, 1950.
The Gay Trapeze, Handcraft Press, 1955.
Inheritance, Paul's Book Arcade, 1962.
Flying to Palmerston, Oxford University Press for Auckland University Press, 1968.

CHARLES SPEAR
Twopence Coloured, Caxton Press, 1951.

C. K. STEAD
Whether the Will is Free, Poems 1954–62, Paul's Book Arcade, 1964.

EDWARD TREGEAR
'Shadows' and Other Verses, Whitcombe and Tombs, 1919.

HONE TUWHARE
No Ordinary Sun, Blackwood and Janet Paul, 1964.

RAYMOND WARD
Settler and Stranger, Caxton Press, 1965.

PAT WILSON
The Bright Sea, Pegasus Press, 1951.

HUBERT WITHEFORD
Shadow of the Flame, Poems 1942–7, Pelorus Press, 1950.
The Falcon Mask, Pegasus Press, 1951.
The Lightning Makes a Difference, Brookside Press, 1962.
A Native, Perhaps Beautiful, Caxton Press, 1967.

K. O. Arvidson, Michael Jackson, and Owen Leeming have not published volumes, but have been widely represented in journals in New Zealand and elsewhere. A selection of Owen Leeming's verse was included in *Recent Poetry in New Zealand*, edited by Charles Doyle.

GLOSSARY OF MAORI WORDS

Ariki	A high chief.
Io	Supreme god in Maori pantheon.
Kahawai	A fish, *Arripis trutta*.
Karaka	A broad-leafed tree, usually about 30 ft. high, common in coastal forest. It is distinctive for its large orange fruit.
Kauri	A forest tree which grows to huge dimensions. Sites of former Kauri forests have been extensively worked for gum.
Kea	A species of native parrot, with olive green plumage and bright vermilion under wings, found only in the South Island, and there mostly in the mountains.
Kowhai	A tree 20–30 ft. high, which in spring is covered in hanging yellow flowers.
Kumara	An edible root known as 'sweet potato'.
Mako	Shark.
Manuka	By far the commonest New Zealand shrub. Seldom more than 12–15 ft. high, it is usually known as 'tea-tree', as the early settlers used its aromatic leaves for brewing.
Marae	An enclosed ground used as a meeting place.
Matai	Black pine found throughout New Zealand in lowland forest.
Maui	Mythical character who, after fabulous feats, sought immortality for mankind, and died between the thighs of the death goddess.
Pakeha	Common term for white New Zealander.
Punga	Tree-fern.
Raupo	Bulrush, used for a variety of domestic purposes.
Rimu	A conifer, sometimes called red pine, with small leaves and pendulous branches as a young tree, that grows to about 100 ft.
Tangi	To mourn, weep, also a funeral ceremony.
Taniwha	A mythical river and seaside monster with man-eating tendencies.
Tapu	Sacred, forbidden.
Tauhinu	A scented shrub, often infesting poor soil.
Tohunga	A Maori priest, acknowledged as an expert in ritual, art, and lore.
Toi-toi	A tall grass, like pampas, with high plumes, sometimes called 'Prince of Wales' feathers'.
Totara	A widely distributed conifer, the tree once most valued by Maoris for the quality of its timber.
Tui	The largest of the honey-eaters native to New Zealand, the tui is predominantly an iridescent black, and is larger than the European blackbird.

INDEX OF AUTHORS

INDEX OF TITLES AND FIRST LINES

Titles are in *italics;* first lines in roman

341

343